Vampire Management

Why your job sucks.

Joseph Phillips

Copy editor: Lisa D. Nuss

Proofreaders: Julie Whitley, Holly Phillips, Courtney Richards

Cover design: David Litwin

Author photo: Hannah Grace Wright

Copyright © 2011 Joseph Phillips

ISBN: 0983970106

ISBN-13: 978-0983970101

For love

CONTENTS

ACKNOWLEDGMENTS

There are many people to whom I owe much in my life: my parents, Don and Virginia Phillips, my brothers Steve, Mark, Sam, and Ben. Thank you to my son Kyle for talking with me about vampires. Thank you to my friends who have encouraged me in this creation: Fred and Carin McBroom, Don Kuhnle, and Amy Alberts. Thank you also to Greg Huebner, Jonathan Acosta, Duane Schoon, and Courtney Richards for the great talks, cigars, and much-needed distractions. I must also thank dear friends Greg Kirkland, Andy, Jo, and Michael Diaczyk, John Texada, Kathy Grandt, Norm and Paulette Tarantola and Kourtnaye Sturgeon for their generosity with wine, friendship, and general camaraderie. Thank you to Andrea Hancock-Deer for her spark. Finally, thank you, reader for giving your time and interest to what I've created. I hope you enjoy it. I hope vampires never find you.

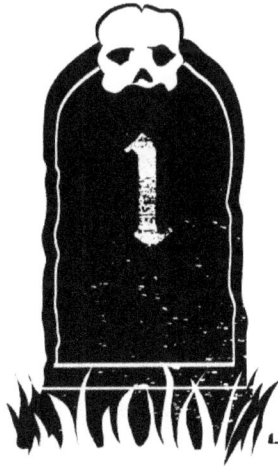

Pains in Your Neck

I'm your manager and I'm a vampire. Allow me to personally welcome you to our organization; we're pleased you've decided to join us in your career. I'm certain you'll be a valuable asset and if there's anything I can do to help, please don't hesitate to ask. My door is always, well, usually, open.

Over the past 97 years I've given that welcome speech, or some variation of it, to thousands of new employees. Okay, I've given that speech minus the vampire business. It's true, I am a vampire. I've travelled the world, seen countries fall apart, witnessed great businesses vanish like a moon on the horizon. I've watched people be born, grow old, and die while I've hardly changed at all. I have made millions of dollars, but I've led a moderate lifestyle to not draw attention to myself.

While I'd really like to snap your neck and drink your blood, I'm not going to; at least not yet. Instead I'm going to do you a favor. I'm going to tell you why your job sucks (pardon the pun). I'm going to reveal how we, vampires, control far more than you think, but aren't as powerful as you're led to believe. I'm going to show you how to deal with vampire managers, how to fight back, and how to make yourself unappealing to blood suckers like me.

Your job sucks for many reasons, but the primary reason is because of vampires like me. We're things that don't really care for you, your colleagues, your goals, action items, or where you think you'll be in five years. You are just another thing we have to deal with on a daily basis. Every day there are meetings, emails, phone calls, conferences, and demands from all directions for vampire managers. For new managers it's an exciting opportunity to lead, but then the realization: it's no opportunity – it's hell. Where is management leading their staff? To retirement, to the promised land, to the next layoff? Leadership, especially vampire leadership, is leading the organization to the purpose of business: to make more money. Leadership at the management level isn't about alignment, motivation, and direction; leadership at the management level is about you doing what I say.

It's little surprise that so many managers are actually vampires. Managers have a rough gig. Let's pretend you're managing 20 people. Each personality in this crowd has issues, drama, desire to get ahead of workmates, they'll do good and bad work, they'll want your attention, and play political games to fit their tiny agenda. That's 20 people for whom you'll have to manage their woes, address their wants and needs, talk to, direct, pretend to motivate, and cajole to do their jobs as adults. Even if you spend just one hour a week managing each person – that's 20 hours of being a glorified babysitter. Spend an hour a week with each person that you'd rather eat than look at and you'll know my hell.

Wait, it gets better. Add to this misery the fact that the managers above you have a crew of managers just like you. These managers, directors, vice-presidents or whatever your company calls them grow to feel about you the same way you do about the 20 people you're managing. And there are the people above them, and above them, and so on. The good news is that the farther up the ladder you climb, the fewer people you have to manage so your life becomes better and better. But that's not you is it? Vampire or not, management bites.

Managers are caught between the layer above and the layer below; that's middle management. Middle management has to take the directives that are passed down to them and then enforce the new rules, policies, bad news, and layoffs directly to the masses. Middle managers are glorified babysitters with dreams of moving onto the next level – of moving on and away from people like you. You might think that's not so bad, that you could hack that for a while. Sure, you probably can. But I've been stuck here in middle management for 97 years in 10 different organizations. I'm resigning, retiring, and returning to my life, my calling, my freedom.

My Life as a Vampire Manager

This is my story, my advice, and the last thing I'll ever do as a vampire manager. This story, this consultation, will be dismissed as a cute little business book. It's not – this is my resignation letter to my firm, The Organization, that I really work for. The Organization is a shadow company that reaches into most businesses, governments, and profitable entities. All vampires are required to work for The Organization – it's like a union, but with higher dues. In The Organization promises have been made, promises broken – and it's all self-serving control from the top down to you. I won't yet delve into the specifics of why I'm quitting, turning rogue, but I've seen the same lies and same deception in your companies as in The Organization. We're not that different.

By the time you're actually reading this I'll likely be dead for good. In the months following these words, I'll probably be hunted down and buried alive under a few tons of cement, left to starve. Or they'll be merciful and just lop off my head. Or they'll use a combination of 100 other methods to kill something that's already dead — none of which will be all that pleasant. But vampire or not, I'm tired of this game, tired of this lack of life, tired of playing by someone else's rules. Then again, maybe this is all a ghost story, entertainment to you — which could be part of our scheme to keep you right where we want you: miserable, living in a cubicle, and earning money for us.

I was recruited in 1849. At the time I was 46 years old, never married, no children. I poured my life into the railroad business. My manager, Hans Goodsby, a vampire, decided I had potential for The Organization and made me everything I am today. I've moved from company to company where The Organization needed me, needed someone to make changes. I've worked in the financial arena, automotive industry, textile factories, health care (*delicious!*), and most recently technology companies. I've worked my way up the ranks from ordinary worker, team leader, and project manager, to the manager of a department. In the world of vampires it's not really about performance, but about who's left in The Organization and what opportunities the void presents.

There are qualifications to being a vampire manager — first, you have to actually be a vampire. For example, I drink blood. I don't melt with holy water, shrink away from crucifixes, or change into flying rodents and vanish into the night. I do, however, avoid the sun. I won't burst into flames in direct sunshine, but sunshine is like a migraine headache all over my body. Sunshine is why I stay so late in the office and why I'm usually there before you drop by for your few hours of labor. I do have fangs, but they grow and shrink based on how hungry I am (visible fangs would make team meetings, interviews, and performance reviews difficult).

Now that vampires are secretly integrated into businesses and governments we have to fit in. This means family life, vacations, seminars, talking about sports, caring about the stock market, and company outings. The life of a vampire used to be pretty good: if you wanted something you just took it. It wasn't hard to get money, to feed, to disappear and start anew in a new city, a new state, or even a new country. The traditional life a vampire is gone. Now it's company picnics, suburbs, and office parties. My life as a vampire is now just ridiculous. And some people actually wonder why I'm so angry?

Can you imagine the heartache we have to go through to eat nowadays? Vampires are now fed like pets, not like the hunters we are. We can't skulk about gouging necks and slurping dinner. In the movies there's always a devilishly good-looking fellow with fangs biting into some young thing's neck. That's not how it's done – at least not anymore. Sure, back in the old days, before rules and regulations, a vampire could slip down a darkened alley and gorge on an unsuspecting Joe or devour some young thing on her way home from the market. I miss the good, old days. Now it's all orderly, rationed, and so business-like that it's hardly fun anymore. It's work – just like your gig.

Your Blood is for Sale

Vampires are organized. We're structured, prepared, managed, controlled, and directed. There are layers and layers of vampire management that define how we interact in all areas of the human-vampire world. It's not about flesh and blood anymore; it's all about money first, doing what you're told second, and then the blood. Priorities are so upside down in your world and in mine. It's about money – not about doing what we're naturally attracted to doing. What is money to a vampire? What's a job to an artist, a writer, a craftsman? You and I aren't living like we're supposed to. Let's do something about this, a partnership of sorts (though I'll be the majority owner).

The Organization influences everything. Imagine thousands of vampires all around you, making decisions for you, determining your future, your life, where you'll work, how you'll contribute, and changing the flow of your day-to-day existence without your knowledge, just your suspicion. Think deeper, blood bag, it's not just you, but everyone you know. The Organization controls it all and sees you as cattle – our cattle. The Organization doesn't care about you; we just see you as dinner walking around.

Face the facts: we're all older than you, smarter than you, and we've been perfecting this approach for a long, long time. The corporate world is an illusion to help us, us vampires, get what we need: the profit for us that surges through *your* veins. While we need blood, your blood, it's not politically correct or financially beneficial to play Dracula. Instead we, like all organizations, play within the boundaries of the law – and we don't get caught when we break it. We might bend the rules a little, but we don't kill our victims immediately. Sure, we take your life away, but we do it one day at a time, one meeting at a time, one paycheck at a time. I suppose you could say we aren't actually taking life from you, you're selling it to us.

The Organization isn't just an entity like a business, but it's more like a club with its members operating in collusion throughout the free market. The Organization has members in all of the largest companies, government agencies, and businesses you'd never suspect. Our members, vampires like me, are tasked with achieving the goals of The Organization, supporting the vision of our host companies, and doing what we're told. Simply put, the health of The Organization is directly related to the health of the vampire. You might get written up for insubordination; vampires get a wooden stake through the heart.

When we make the host company profitable, The Organization is profitable. Profits allow us to buy what we need: blood. That's right, The Organization purchases your blood, which they prefer to call product, and then it's distributed to each of us. You're probably wondering how we purchase all that blood, I mean product. It's actually simple. Ever wondered about the plasma center in your neighborhood? Ever had a nurse draw two vials of blood instead of one for alleged medical testing? Ever donated blood out of the goodness of your thumpin' little heart? There you go.

Vampires need a few pints a weeks to survive, but a gallon a week is ideal. We're fed through a variety of options: delivery through courier services, corner blood banks, doctor and dentist visits, anonymous offices, and even certain drive-through restaurants. It's all around and you've never seen it. I know it's tough to think about me, your manager, drinking blood in the "World's Greatest Dad" coffee mug, but that's the way this works. Sure, there are some pretty boys who won't put the stuff on their lips and take the product through an intravenous bag, but that's so hygienic. Most of us, especially those of us in management, need the product on our tongues – it's the only reminder of how exciting this life used to be.

Vampire Hierarchy

The Organization is divided into three primary chunks of structure. At the very top-level of the structure, the executive layer, are the real decision makers. This is the layer above me where the oldest vampires operate. These are the spooky vampires with the money, the luxurious life, and who create the most product. These executives have come into power by killing off their competition and forming alliances.

The executives have been around for so long, since medieval times, that they just can't relate to the world you and I live in. They don't get the idea of bills, taxes, personal time off, and living for weekends and holidays. In their human memories things were much simpler, not at all like life today. These old souls might be wise based on what they've experienced through their infected lives, but they don't understand the difficulties management and employees can have with their demands and expectations. Ah, but they don't care – they don't have to – if I don't do as I'm told then someone else will.

Below me you'll find the drones of The Organization. These are the managers in training, the youngest vampires that are smart enough to do what they're told, dream of being something bigger in The Organization, and work, work, work to make money, money, money. These are the employees that probably make you insane: they always get the plushest assignments, seem to be an eternal frat boy or sorority girl, and they're smart, good-looking, and optimistic. These drones can work in operational roles for years and years. Some may move up the management chain while others may fill a need and stay right where they are.

Vampire management doesn't care about employees. Vampire management only cares about accomplishment. Think back to the pyramids: it wasn't purely slave labor that got those things built. It still took organization, direction, oversight, and muscle to get the people to carve, move, stack, and position those rocks just so. Now fast-forward to Henry Ford – again, management was oversight in the assembly line of cars. An individual had to understand the process and then oversee that people were doing the correct work in the correct manner. Now leap to any construction, manufacturing, or other work that requires physical muscle to complete: a manager is needed to ensure that the work is completed as planned.

Now let's examine businesses like banks, insurance companies, any government agency, or any work that requires brains over brawn. How do you manage brainpower? You create processes to bring about a specific result. You create checklists to direct thought patterns. You have meetings to communicate so that people understand what you want them to do. When muscles are involved there's an immediate delivery of results, when brains are involved it's much more complicated because management can't see what you're thinking about. Unless you're a vampire.

For a vampire the role of management is simple: get things done or else. This order can be executed in any action that works: inspiration, motivation, bribes, threats, cajoling, reorganization, and worse. We are competitive not for the good of your organization but for our life in The Organization. There are expectations and demands on vampire managers; if we don't make our divisions - your companies - profitable, then The Organization suffers and we'll suffer all the same. That's why fear is a great motivator for vampire managers – we're afraid, so you're going to be afraid, too. We are, as you might have guessed, a pain in the neck.

Those of us in management, and there are thousands, are caught between the executives in your organization and the executives in The Organization. Care to guess which one we dread the most? Human CEOs can berate us, embarrass us, threaten to fire us, but it's the vampires in The Organization that we cannot displease. If we turn a bad quarter, even if it's the damn economy, there are consequences. Forget about bonuses and pay raises – I'm talking about consequences that can mean starving for a few weeks, hours in a suntan booth, and other tortures.

One of the things you don't hear about vampires, because we don't want you to know, is that we feel pain to a higher degree than humans. Most of our senses are heightened as vampires; we can see, hear, even taste better than any human, but this also means we feel much more intently. You stub your toe and it might ache for awhile – we stub a toe and it's like breaking a leg. Pain is evident in all that we do – just one of the reasons why vampires make great managers, because we're generally not happy creatures.

Because management is about getting things done you first have to know what you want to accomplish. You have to know what the work's purpose is. Some might say the point of business, of doing the work of the business, is to make money. Sure, that's Management 101. Work and money are related, but you're missing the joy of the work. Money is just the byproduct of satisfying the work's purpose. A business's purpose is to fulfill a need or seize a market opportunity. You can see the purpose in building a house, in hosting a conference, in manufacturing farm equipment. If you can't see the purpose in the day-to-day work you perform you'll probably feel frustrated, manipulated, and like your life's being wasted.

What I've learned in my life as a vampire is that most people are indeed wasting their lives because they can't see the purpose of their work. Every action you take must have personal purpose or it's meaningless to you. If it's meaningless, then you're not motivated to do the work – your spirit suffers, your heart longs for something with personal value, and your motivation collapses. Knowing what you know now about The Organization, is it any surprise that vampire managers delight in your misery? The Organization won't allow me to kill you, eat you, or immediately drink your blood, but I can torture you through pointless action items, waste-of-time meetings, redundancy, demands for reports that I'll never read, and hours of training for something I'll probably never have you do. I balance your insanity with just enough productivity to keep things profitable.

Your Job is a Grave Matter

I imagine that when you were a young person, a parent, a teacher, or even a priest told you that you needed to stay in school for as long as you could. They probably told you to learn all that you can, to earn as many degrees as you could, and to be something significant like a doctor, an attorney, or a businessman. That's nice, but were any of those things what your heart wanted to do? Maybe, but probably not. What you were really experiencing, shadowed in their well-intended advice, was their regret for what they wished they'd accomplished – financial dreams.

Most people don't know what they want to do with their lives, so they either pursue careers that will guarantee them a nice income or they pursue jobs that'll help them get by until they discover what they really want to do. I'm not criticizing you, it's what I did before I became what I am. Young people make the mistake of going on to college not with the intent of discovering the joy of being educated, but with the intent of getting a good job. A good job provides the illusion of financial security, which can provide the necessities of living, material goods, car payments, and a financed lifestyle which leaves little money in savings. For many people the more they earn the more they will spend which in turn causes individuals to embrace the jobs they hate.

You may have already made this self-discovery. I picture you waking one dawn with the realization that your job sucks. Your job has no personal meaning, no personal value, but you have to get in there, are expected to do these mindless tasks, deal with people you don't really like, and create forms, complete processes, and make someone else wealthy. You're doing this not because you love your job, but because you need the money. You're doing this to provide for your family, to have money to pay for that nice car, a place to live, shoes for little feet, and to stick just a little back for some cloudy, rainy day when you're old and gray.

You can't quit this job because you need what the job provides. The thought of your employment ending scares you nearly to death. The thought of looking for a job somewhere else confirms that the hell you know is better than hell you don't. You are scared of what life without this steady hell will bring. So rather than gamble for something better, something that your soul longs to do, you keep on doing what you despise. You lie to yourself and make promises that one day you'll get to be a writer, an actor, a painter, a musician, a teacher – or whatever calling and purpose whispers to you in your dreams and in pointless meetings.

And that's how we have you. Vampire management keeps you scared of leaving for something better. Vampire management uses that fear, we love that fear, to keep you doing whatever we tell you to do. Your fear empowers us to treat you however we damn well please. You fear not having enough money to live on, you fear change, you fear rejection, you fear failure and success, and you fear not having the nice things you've grown accustomed to in your life. You're too scared to leave and too scared to do something about the misery we create for you – because if you speak up you just might be without your job, without your paycheck, and then you'll be starting all over. You're trapped and there's nothing you can about it – as far as you know.

It delights me to finally tell you that there are things worse than death. When you live your life in fear you might as well unbutton that collar, lean your head way back, and wait for my fangs. You're not living; you're merely existing. Death will find you one day – and then it'll be too late and your dreams, desires, passion, and purpose will be lost. Take some advice from a vampire: your life is precious and I envy it. You can keep being miserable while trading your life for a paycheck and promises or you can fight back. You can take actions to change your life, to find joy, and do something that I'll never do again: live.

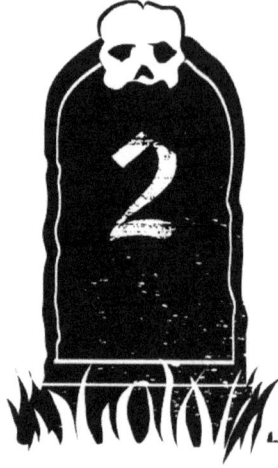

What Your Heart Wants and Needs

Your job sucks for many different reasons, but the heart of the matter is that your job sucks because of you. I know, that's a bit tough, but stick around for a hundred years or so and you'll be mean, too. You are the primary reason why your job sucks, why you're unhappy, and why you are where you are. You can't blame your parents, your education, or your obligations forever. Well, I suppose you can blame everyone else – and yes, they may have had some influence over your life - but let's be reasonable, this is *your* life.

I'm not saying that you need to tell 'em all to go to hell and go live on a sailboat. All your family, friends, and even colleagues are part of your life – these are people you love and tolerate, but they are not your entire life. These are people that you share time with and that you choose to love, but they are just part of your purpose. I know it's important for fleshy things like you to feel loved, to feel invested in others, and to feel love for others. I remember loving. I remember caring how others feel. It's a good feeling to know that you're cared for, loved, and admired.

You might reason that you do the work you do so that you can provide for those you love. You might reason that your suffering is almost saint-like because you're toughing it out at a job you hate so that your family may have a life that you just can't. Every day you trudge into the office and endure the misery in exchange for your pay, your benefits, weekends, and a couple weeks of vacation a year. You willingly give up your whole life to provide for others, to pay for that minivan, and to feed tiny mouths. You're such a martyr; get off the cross so we can use the wood.

Do you really think these people that you care for and that care for you want you to be miserable? Is a life of misery an example you want to set for your children? Do you want to teach your children that life is rotten, that they too will one day suffer, trade their purpose for a life of gloom and a paycheck? I doubt it. I bet you have aspirations for your friends, spouse, and children. I bet you see them living out their dreams, finding their purpose, and going on to do great things. Didn't you have some dreams and purpose once too? Didn't you hear a calling when you were younger?

That calling is still there, but your heart is beating so loudly from fear that you can't hear it anymore. Quit being so scared, face your fears, and fight back the vampires. I'll help.

Reflecting on Needs and Wants

A vampire's life is really pretty boring. The passions and desires I've had have long since faded into the twilight. As a vampire, my needs are simple: your blood, a few hours of sleep, and something to occupy another day of eternity. You might think that'd be a great opportunity – all that time and energy, but trust me, after fifty or so years with no passion you're ready for something different. It's the boredom that shifts us into evil things – it's why we meddle, play office politics, and strangle your ambitions.

Vampires are jealous and disgusted with people like you. We're jealous of the potential that you have to excel, to create, to go and do whatever you'd like. You have the abilities to continue living, to embrace your passion, and to feel the thrill of achievement, of learning, and to be excited with creating. Vampires don't feel that thrill – and we're constantly mourning the loss of opportunity. Don't you see why I hate you? You can start living however and doing whatever you want, but vampires don't feel passion at all. Still, with the whole world before you, you choose to come to a job you despise. With the whole world before you, you don't take the risk to even try your desire because of the fear you might have to drive an older car, live in a different zip code, or do without the toys your friends have.

Cars, houses, designer clothes, and other luxuries are just things. These are distractions – things to which you're emotionally attached, to hide the regret of not doing what you should be doing. Does an expensive car zip you to the office, a place you don't really want to be, faster than a less expensive car? Does the overpriced mini-mansion keep you warmer than a reasonable home in the suburbs? Do the clothes with the fancy labels keep you warmer? You might argue that those higher-priced items do keep you warmer, safer, and more comfortable than the cheaper items. But these are wants – the ancillary items that make your miserable life tolerable. Which would you rather have: a joyful, simple life doing what your heart desires or a miserable life numbed by a fat paycheck?

Here's some good news: these are not exclusive choices. You can do what your heart desires and still make a living. There's nothing wrong with making money – I know – but there's plenty wrong with wasting your life on something you despise only to make money. I'm not promising that if you go and become a painter, a musician, a writer, or whatever is calling you that you'll be wealthy. (And never trust promises from a vampire.) All I'm saying is that if you go and do what you need to do, what you should be doing, you'll be joyful, have a more fulfilling life, and be a better example to your family, your friends, and even the colleagues you leave behind with me.

What you need and what you want are usually two different things. I'm sure you've read up on Maslow and his Hierarchy of Needs. As a quick refresher, Abraham Maslow, a professor of psychology who wanted counselors and psychologists to focus on the positive aspects of people rather than their negative traits, said that humans have five fundamental needs that shape your actions, beliefs, and ultimately your values:

- **Physiological** – you have a need to have your hunger, thirst, and sleep satisfied
- **Safety** – you need to feel and actually be safe
- **Social** – you have a need for friendship, admiration of others, love, and companionship
- **Esteem** – you have a need to feel pride in yourself, value in your contributions to the world, and a sense of achievement
- **Self-actualization** – you have a need to fulfill your life's purpose, your calling, (the essence of what I've been talking to you about)

Each need is contingent on the need just prior to it. In other words, you're probably not real interested in making new friends if you've not had food or water for a few days. In order to climb up the hierarchy you must satisfy each need. The pinnacle of the hierarchy is self-actualization, which is the realization and fulfillment of what you're in this world to achieve. Vampires have a physiological need that directly aligns with our self-actualization: we need to feast and it's why we exist. We cheat that way.

Maslow addresses needs as the things you must have in your life. But you're often consumed by wants, aren't you? Wants are the emotional longings that drive many of your actions. Think about the things people want: expensive cars, exotic vacations, hedonistic activities with beautiful people, wealth, and pleasure. Wants aren't always bad things: joy, love, abundance for family and friends, health, and real security. Wants are different than needs because needs must be met or there can be physical and mental consequences. Wants don't have to be met, they often are not met, and the only ramification can be disappointments. Needs are attached to the demand for living – while wants are attached to the emotions vampires no longer enjoy.

There comes a point in your life, in everyone's life, where the prioritization of wants diminishes in relation to the guarantee of needs. There's a natural balance of finding comfort in the knowledge of meeting many of your needs in exchange for giving up your wants. For example, you might forgo the wanted short-lived pleasure of smoking, eating unhealthy, and being a bum on the street corner in exchange for the healthy diet, a safe place to sleep, and the development of esteem.

It's this trade of time and energy for monies that also allow you to satisfy some of your wants, too. You can afford to finance the nice car, the bigger house, the vacations on the credit cards, and take on more and more debt to get what you immediately want. The immediate gratification, the financing of satisfaction, may offer immediate pleasure, but can provide long-term misery. It's part of The Organization's goal to bleed you dry, to keep you earning, to keep you under my control. The Organization wants to keep you in debt, to keep you burdened with wants, and to keep a foot on your throat so you'll only ever climb so high in Maslow's Hierarchy. We need you enslaved to your wants and moderately fulfilled in your needs.

Values to Count On

If you want to break out from vampire management you first have to define your values. The values I'm talking about are the things, people, conditions, and elements in your life that are most valuable to you. For a vampire this is pretty easy: we value the product, dark places, and making your life a misery. Your values may be things like loving your friends and family, giving your time and energy to something that's worthy of your talents, and doing work that's meaningful. Only you can know your values and these can change over time, but you first have to know what's important to you before you can achieve it.

Understanding your values isn't that different than what business analysts do in an organization. You know business analysts, right? They are the pesky, nerdy, question-filled people that dig into requirements for projects, opportunities, and problems. Business analysis is the process of finding what needs to be created and determining if it's worth the cost of the creation. Business analysts examine the business rationale of spending organizational money in relation to the return on investment. Lots of new vampires work well as business analysts.

You have to play the role of business analyst in your life. Ask yourself lots of questions to dig down to what's really important to you. You need to examine your personal life, your professional life, your current life status, and where you want to go in the future. It's perfectly human to want nice things – I did and sometimes still do. Nice things are comfortable, pretty to look at, wonderful to experience – but nice things often come with a price you may not be able to afford. The want I'm really talking about here are not just the want of things, but the wants of conditions.

Imagine your ideal life. For me, if I were still alive, it'd be a beautiful woman that loves me as much as I'd love her. We'd have a rustic cabin high in the Appalachian Mountains – where we both would work as artists and raise our seven children. I'd spend the morning perfecting my craft and the occasional afternoons perfecting my fly fishing. Evenings would be homework, bed time stories, and then a glass of wine by the fire. No television, just books and good music. But that's my ideal life that'll never happen. What's your ideal life that certainly can happen? You are still alive.

That's fantasy. Life is rarely ideal – you probably won't get everything you want and need all the time. You'll get sick, people will die, things won't work out. But there's also great joy in life – you'll fall in love, you'll have good friends, you'll do great work. There are highs and lows; focus on one or the other and it'll be amazing what you'll discover. When you're looking for four-leaf clovers you don't think about apple trees. In other words, what you focus on, the vision in your mind's eye, is what you'll find more often than not.

If you don't have a definition for your values, if you don't have a vision for where you want to go, if you don't have demands for your wants and desires you'll probably end up like me: unhappy, feeling lonely, and nearly trapped in a shell of a life. To find joy in your life you must define what's important to you. You must find someone to love, find meaningful work, and have goals to work toward. You need to determine what you want and what you need in your life. Once you've defined what you want and need, you must prioritize your wants and needs – make your own hierarchy; screw Maslow.

Your Job Sucks Because of Debt

Put on some smooth jazz, pour yourself a glass of red wine, and write up your list of wants and needs. You might put all of your wants in one column and then all your needs in another. With a little time you could prioritize each list of what's most important to you; with a bit more time you could even merge the two lists together to create one big definition of all that you want and need. Fascinating. But what will you do with it? Will you tape that list to your bathroom mirror, tuck it into your wallet, or hide it away to daydream about from time to time?

If you're like most people that have worked for me, a long list of dreams, wants, and desires really doesn't matter. I say that because people won't ever achieve their wants and needs without making some sacrifices. I gave you some foreshadow to this obvious truth: your job sucks because of debt. Your job sucks because you're working like a vampire without being a vampire. You're just existing with nothing left over for achievement in the things that really matter to you. How will you ever achieve the things on your list of wants and needs if you've no savings, no time, and no energy to do so? What's your plan, to borrow more so you can buy your way to happiness? It doesn't work that way. You're mortgaged to the grave – and sometimes beyond.

If you were brave enough to create a list of wants and needs I'd wager that three of your needs are to pay off debt, a career goal like a certification or new job, and to lose weight. Losing weight I can help you with immediately – though you probably won't like the everlasting results or my approach. Finding a new job, we'll talk about that coming up. For now it's the big need you have: pay off debt. Here's an interesting question: why are you in debt? What did you promise to do tomorrow in order to have today?

Some of your debt might be justified – medical bills, education loans, and maybe even a house payment. When you owe companies money you are really paying with your life. You're smart, I'm assuming. If you borrow $175,000 from the biggest bloodsuckers, a bank, to purchase a house, I hope you don't think you're only paying back the $175,000. Who knows what interest rate you have on the price tag of that beautiful home, but let's pretend it's a measly six percent for 30 years. You'll be paying $377,640 for that house. Sometimes it's better to do without, to make do, in order to have what's really important.

House payments are one thing, but what other debt is draped around your neck? What credit card bills, car payments, and department store cards are haunting your financial security? I dare you to find out how much you really owe, interest, past due payments, and total liabilities. How much would you have to pay right now to be free and clear of all debt? How much would you have to pay each month to be free in one year? What about in five years? Staggering? I hope not. If you're a vampire you take forever to pay off loans, but you're not a vampire (yet) and your time is ticking away. The debt you owe robs you of doing what's most important to you. The debt you owe is paid for with more than just dollars.

When you a carry a big stack of bills you feel trapped in your employment. You might hear some folks talk about golden handcuffs – or they can't afford to leave their job. What they really mean is that they can't afford to quit and maintain their present lifestyle. I've seen employees, miserable employees, grind out their forty hours of work to earn their pay. Then their pay is evaporated by bills and they've nothing left to show for their efforts. They are so in debt that their paycheck is gone before it's even deposited in their bank. These are the folks, maybe just like you, that hate their job not because of a vampire management, but because of a scarier monster they've created: debt.

Leaving Vampire Managers by Killing Debt Demons

If you want to get away from vampire managers you need to get away from debt demons too. When you're buried in debt it's more challenging to leave a job where a vampire is in charge. If you're free of debt then you have the flexibility to leave the vampire, pursue your dreams, and even start your own business. Vampire managers love for you to be in debt because it's tougher, if not impossible, for you to leave your current job.

Before you can achieve your wants and needs you'll need to get your obligations in order. This means you'll have to pay what you owe in order to move forward to what you want *and* need. Let's be real clear here; you do not want to kill one debt monster in order to create a new one. One of your wants shouldn't be to pay off one loan so that you can finance a new car. That's not killing the debt monster at all – that's letting the monster live on and rule your life. To kill the debt monster means that you *do not owe*.

Gasp! The horror! Yes, I mean you don't owe car payments, taxes, a mortgage or credit card bills. Debt, all debt, keeps you enslaved. When you owe a company you owe The Organization. Owing an amount, no matter how small or manageable, can limit your ability to put time, money, and energy into what you want *and* need to do in your life. You may have to live with the debt monster for awhile, but this doesn't mean you make friends with him.

The first step in killing your personal debt demon is to stop feeding him. Don't generate more debt while you're trying to get out of debt. Quit adding bills! No, you cannot finance a time-share vacation. No, you cannot hire a maid to clean your house. No, you cannot lease a new car. Stop spending money or the debt won't ever go away. You'd think this would be an easy enough task to grasp, but I've seen it for as long as I can remember. People start killing off debt, have a bit of accessible cash, and then they reason they can start spending again.

The second step in erasing debt is to reduce your bills. You probably aren't going to like this one, but I don't care. You'll only do it if you're serious anyway – and since most of you are lazy, scared lumps of flesh nothing's going to change. But if you're one of the smart ones, you'll take this uncomfortable step: get rid of monthly service fees. This means you turn off your cable television. Turn off your high-speed internet. Turn off any monthly fee that's related to entertainment. If you're not going to die or starve, then it's a monthly fee you can do without. Get rid of it.

Reducing your bills doesn't mean that you have to get rid of everything you spend money on. You still need to eat, but you don't need to eat at the fanciest restaurants every night of the week. You don't need the five-dollar coffees, the expensive lunches, and the tickets for the ballgames, the theatre, and the rock concerts. You need to stop spending money.

Once you've stopped spending money and reduced your monthly outgoing expenses you can really dig in and pay towards killing your debt. The money that you would have spent on the monthly services, on the fancy coffees, and the front-row tickets now go to the capital you owe. You no longer pay the minimum due, but you attack the maximum due. Find the bill with the highest interest rate, probably some stupid credit card. This is the bill you'll pay the most towards until it's completely paid off.

All of your other bills are paid the minimum amount due, not ignored, but with the funds you've freed from your budget you attack the largest, most expensive debt until it's dead and gone. Then you take the same strategy and attack the next chunk of debt. And then the next. And so on. You do without so that you can have more later. By freeing yourself from debt you've given some purpose to a job that you despise. By finding purpose in a job that's not enjoyable you're turning against The Organization and starting to set yourself free.

Hell is Other People

Jean-Paul Sartre penned the famous line "hell is other people" in his play "No Exit." Never mind his socialist and Marxist beliefs, he was spot on with what we all know: other people can make your life a living hell. "Hell is other people" proves true when you work for the boss who demands complex reports that he'll only complain about and never read. Or when your manager forces you to work weekends and late nights instead of being with your family. Or when you've no choice but to tolerate the boss who rants at you for every tiny mistake but allows his favorite to get away with murder. When vampire managers recruit new workers we aren't concerned with their personal hygiene, their personal habits that may infringe on your peace of mind, or their abilities to drive their coworkers insane. We're only focused on getting someone with just enough competence to fill a need to help us be more profitable. We can't pay too much for talent because labor digs into our profit margin. That's we why often hire the people that have the lowest competence-to-contribution value. If we wanted to hire the people with the most competence, the most professionalism, the most ability to succeed we'd have to give up too much cash.

So instead we hire people that will get the job done for the least amount of money. Unfortunately, these people are often the same folks that have the least amount of courtesy for their office mates. These are the underperformers, the workers that take credit for your hard work, or the drama queens that cry on your desk and shoulder. The interest of The Organization is profit – not your comfort, peace, or enjoyment. Trust me, as much as you can; I don't enjoy hanging out with these people anymore than you do. The difference is, of course, I usually don't have to, you do.

Some managers may tell you that they are always looking for individuals that are the best in the organization. This is a little white lie. Managers are looking for individuals that will cost the least and provide the most. We don't need the expensive Harvard grad when the community college drop-out can satisfy the need. All businesses exist not to provide employment, but to make money. In the last few years the concept of profitability has become as evil as vampires. Profitability is why you have a job. Profitability is why companies are launched. People don't risk their life savings to open a business so that people like you can have jobs – the goal is to make money first. It's not greed, it's risk and reward. Entrepreneurs can lose it all, and often do. Employees have little invested in comparison to the men and women who have taken a chance to do something besides work for things like me.

Still, that knowledge doesn't make the people who sit all around you more tolerable.

Managing Vampire Envy

Some employees want to be just like me. They want to be in charge, have the nice salary, and drain the lives out of others. While they may not realize what it's like to be a vampire, they want the perceived power and strength that comes with it. These achievers will do anything they can to reach the next level, and then the next level, and the level after that. Ambition is a shot of dopamine that fuels them on to the degree, title, certification, or the next rung of the corporate ladder.

Nothing wrong with wanting a better life, that is until you are expected to crush everyone that gets in your way. The desire for power and achievement is a dangerous drug when you're working in the command of a vampire. When I see a person like this my life suddenly gets much, much easier. No longer do I have to push others to do what they're supposed to do. No longer do I have to manage problems and drama. No longer do I have to waste my time putting out fires and reviewing work. With a vampire envious employee in my ranks I can get them to do all the things I don't want to – and more.

A few years ago I had a victim, I mean an employee, named Susan. Susan was power-hungry. She understood office politics, knew how to align forces, and play games to get what she wanted. She was first to volunteer for any assignment, would arrive early and stay late. She'd do as I asked without exception. Susan wanted what I had: power over you. So I simply directed her to make certain that people like you were doing what was asked. Susan became my spy, my favorite employee, and a pawn to get you and your colleagues to actually work.

Was she popular? No. Her colleagues saw her as a suck-up. But that only made her work harder for me. All it took was a couple of months designating her as "The Employee of the Month" and her ego was fed and their spirits were crushed. It was easy to watch her attitude soar, to watch her recruit weaker employees to help her with her causes, and to see her demeanor change from an office worker to a would-be vampire. She was determined to climb up the ranks, but she never realized that I was standing between her and her corporate goals. She'd never leave because she was just too valuable to me.

After a year of having her do my bidding I simply gave her a new title, like project manager, and a tiny bump in pay. Her resume was bolstered and her desire to please me was renewed. While she didn't actually climb the ranks in the company, she saw the tiny control and tiny pay raises as signs of things to come. Of course, I also lied to her and kept her believing that there was an opportunity when one didn't exist. It's not hard to manipulate those with vampire envy when you're a vampire. In fact, it's not hard to manipulate anyone when you know what they want. If you understand what other people want and they believe that you can help them get it, you can own that person forever – or until they discover what you really are, but then it's too late.

I say it's too late because there's something wonderfully awful that happens to people with vampire envy: they can't quit their desire. The more they want to be the manager, but can't get what they want, the harder they'll work to try to move on up. In their minds they're caught between the devil and the unemployment line. They reason that they've already invested so much time and energy in their career that they can't turn away now. They reason that if they go somewhere else they'll be starting at the bottom of the stack – and they'll have years of hard labor to get back where they are now.

If I've done my job right, and I usually do, these folks fall right into the category of not being able to afford to leave. Years of incremental raises in pay equate to more bills, more toys, and the aforementioned debt. Usually, the more a person earns the more the person will owe. And the more these envious workers owe, the more they have to earn to just maintain their lives. People that want to be like me never will be – they're too valuable to be promoted.

Life in the Flesh Farm

One of the biggest insults to human nature was the invention of the cubicle. Why not just call it a barn stall, throw in some hay, and let you live like an animal? From a manager's point of view, cubicles make perfect sense. The cost per square foot is relatively low: practically nonexistent construction costs, shared overhead lights, and everyone has the same type of office. Well, everyone but managers, of course. You and your colleagues are out there in the cube farm. Want to know a secret? Vampire managers don't call it the cube farm – we call it the flesh farm.

From my perspective, as a vampire, cubicles are more valuable than just the cost savings. When you and your peers are herded into your cubes I can see what you're doing anytime and all the time. You may have heard of management by walking around? That's MBA-talk for the manager being visible to better manage the office team. For me, management by walking around means that I can see what you're up to with just a simple stroll through the office. Life in the flesh farm means there's little privacy for phone calls, no opportunity for moonlighting, no napping, or plotting your exit from my domain. When I can keep my eyes on you you're more likely to do what I want you to do. I know it feels like a prison – that's the idea.

Cubicles keep your spirits and dreams in check. After all, how can you ever realistically excel when everyone around you has the same square footage to operate? You and your peers are boxed in –an artistic metaphor for how business wants to keep you and your ambitions in check. Stroll through any office building and it'll probably look just like the one you're trapped in: a systematic grid of navy blue cloth walls, tan desks, and black mesh chairs. Every workplace, your office or the one you think you'd like to go to, is just like this. Sure, there are a few oddball companies out there with fancy, open-air work spaces, but look closer and you'll see they're just as confining as the flesh farm you're in now.

Cubicles keep everyone equal and uniform. In today's world, office space uniformity and the appearance of equality is important. Look at children's soccer games and report cards — scores and honor rolls have gone away because no one wants to be a loser. Office workers, probably someone just like you, might get their feelings hurt if you work hard and get an actual office with a door. Or someone might get suspicious if you can shut the door to your office and think in silence as you crank out those ten-hour days. No, no. Everyone, you and the mouth breather next to you, must be equal. You all shall have the same space, the same desk set, and the same office supplies. After all, it's easier to manage a crew of clones and drones than an office full of individuals.

Life Among the Undead Colleagues

Because your job is undesirable and less than what you had planned for your life, it's safe to assume that the same is true for most everyone else you work with. It's true that for some people what you consider the daily grind is the ideal life — it's their purpose and vision for exactly how they wanted their life to be. Poor souls. But for you and most of your colleagues, what you do each day is far less than perfect. You live for two days a week and maybe two weeks a year — the rest is moments of your life that you sell to merely exist. Vampires love it.

You know the drill. You roll out of bed and hit the shower. Down some coffee, maybe get the kids out the door, and then you line up for your daily commute to a place you really don't want to be. It's asinine jokes on the radio and the same songs you've heard for years all the way to your designated parking space. Then you trudge into your cube, check your email, and it's another day of your life. Meetings about meetings, action items, and checklists guide your thoughts and actions, every day, over and over. It's the same today as yesterday and will be tomorrow. Tuesday and Thursday are indistinguishable by little more than what's for lunch.

After work you might have to deal with the kiddos or meet up with friends for dinner and drinks. You'll commiserate about your day, sigh and gasp at the thought of more days in the office, and then it is brain-numbing television, bed, and setting the alarm clock for more of the same tomorrow. Some of you might lie in bed and count down the number of days until Friday afternoon, or the number of weeks until vacation, or the number of years until you can retire and tell me to go to hell. Good for you – but it's sad really. What'll you do after the weekend? What'll you do after your vacation? Back to work. And retirement? You're assuming you'll actually make it out alive. Your life doesn't start when you leave work – your life is happening all the time.

People like you might as well be zombies – except you'd be less valuable to people like me. You're not living, but you're not really dead either. You're going through the motions with hopes of one day escaping my lair, of one day getting on with your life. Until then, you reason, this is what you'll have to do in hopes of something better. The problem with that logic is that you might die any day – it happens all the time, I know. One day you're the undead and the next you really are dead. Your life, unlike mine, doesn't go on forever.

Quit wasting your breath doing something you despise. You'll never live as long as I have, you'll never see all that I have – and you'll never feel the lust I have for your opportunity. Do you really think I love spending my time in that office? Do you really think I'd rather be there than curled up in a crypt somewhere? That's about the only thing we have in common – neither of us wants to be there. The difference is that I have to be, you do not. If you don't show up you can go onto something else, if I don't show up I'll be gone forever.

You might not be like your colleagues, but you can see that you might become one of them. I dare you to look around the office. Talk with your friends. Ask people what they think of their job. Notice how many of them smile and tell you how wonderful their job is. I'd wager not many. I've worked in many different organizations and a common theme is that people are unhappy. Sure, it's work, it's hard, it's tedious, but that's not the reason people are unhappy. Do you think Monet's paintings weren't hard, tedious work? Do think he hated what he was creating? Hard, tedious work can be wonderfully rewarding work, but only if it's the right work for you. Working around hundreds of people who aren't happy is infectious: stick around and their misery will eat your brains – but save your heart, that's for me.

Your Job Sucks Because of Other People

In certain management philosophies it's believed that adults know how to work together and can put aside petty inconveniences, bad habits, and other annoyances. These theories posit that adults can operate as a team for the betterment of the company – the profits of the executives and shareholders. People will work together because that's what is expected of them. Of course, these philosophies were probably developed by some ancient college professor that never worked next to the idiots that you do.

It's not just the inconsiderate beings that can make your life hell; it's also the cloud of communal despair that hangs over your cubicles. If you're not happy with management's decisions, the type of work you're doing, or the ridiculous, redundant processes, you're probably not alone. Management, human management, often fails to see how expensive misery is for their company. If you're miserable, others are too – and misery loves company, and when there's company there's chatter and complaints. Chatter and complaints equate to lots of time away from why the company exists: to make money.

Some managers may genuinely care about your misery, about the irrational colleagues, and about your happiness. These saints may recall what it was once like to be stuck in a cubicle with unsavory colleagues. Their empathy doesn't mean that your life will become better – they may be powerless to do anything about your discomfort. Their job is still to make certain you get things done, to make certain your time is profitable. You might think human resources is the place to go, but for most organizations human resources has become the legal office to protect the interest of the profitable, not your emotions and sanity.

These people that grind on your nerves are magnified because you know this job, this employment, is what you must endure in to provide for yourself and your family. That's not living, that's just surviving. Here's the truth: your entire life will ache, not just your time at work, until you make peace and escape the despair.

Escaping the Living Dead

The good news is that you're not quite undead – you're just on your way. The very act of reading this book, of taking some initiative is proof enough there's still a pulse inside you. But how strong is that heartbeat? When you're just a lump of flesh, going through our defined processes and actions, you're not living for you – you're selling your life. If you want to escape, if you want to really live, you need to do four things:

- Define **what you want to do with your life.** Notice it's not what things you want to acquire, what places you want to live, and how much you weigh. Life is for doing – define the activities that will make your life worth living. Yes, I'm talking about your occupation, your aspirations, but I'm also talking about physical activity. You need to move that fat, pasty body of yours; run, swim, jump rope, take a hike – whatever. Your body is made for moving, not for just sitting on your wide ass all day. Define what you'll do in your life on a broad scale and on an immediate scale.

- **Define things that are blocking your actions.** Chances are the biggest element that's keeping you from your definition of success is you. Are you afraid of success? Afraid of what others may say when you take a chance and break free? Don't be afraid of success, don't be afraid of others – especially when you're already working for a vampire. You probably, deep down, think you don't deserve to do what you want – you think you're not strong enough, smart enough, or experienced enough. I'm an evil being, but I'm honest: you can do more than you think. If you do the work, the effort, the dedication, you'll deserve whatever you get.

- **Define your plan.** So you know what you want to do and you know what's stopping you, now you need to define exact actions to make these definitions a reality. You must know exactly how to get from where you are today to where you want to be tomorrow. Clearly define the vision of what you'll do in your life. Clearly define how you'll remove the roadblocks between today and your future. When you know what you really want and you know how to get there the next step is nearly magical.

- **Get to work.** What? Surely you didn't believe that if you just think real hard about things they'd come true? That's preposterous; you're smarter than that. Once you've defined your plan you need to get to work executing your plan. Quit moping – this is work and it'll probably require more hours of effort than you're already selling to things like me. If you don't want to do the work, you'll never get what you think you want in your life. And you won't deserve it; you'll deserve to be where you are now: a miserable, mush-brain professional selling their life a day, a dollar at a time.

Have you ever been in a cave? No, not a cave where vampires are lurking in the shadows (at least not that you know), but I'm talking about a normal, everyday cave. Inside this normal cave are stalagmites and stalactites – rocky columns on the floor and ceiling that have been built by droplets of minerals over thousands of years – one drip of water at a time. These formations didn't happen in a week's time, a year's time, or even in your lifetime, but over thousands of years of persistent, tiny actions have created these solid, amazing sculptures. I'm not saying your plan should take thousands of years, but rather you must take consistent steady actions.

There's a Japanese philosophy called Kaizen. Kaizen is often used in change management processes by applying tiny, almost imperceptible changes to bring about eventual, significant changes. Kaizen, like cave formations, require tiny, consistent action to bring about the desired result. You can use Kaizen in your plan to get from where you are now to where you want to go in your life. The secret to achievement and change is the application of steady, consistent actions. Persistence is the key to almost anything you want to accomplish; you don't give up when you're trying to climb out of a grave.

Vampires are Sociopaths

I trust you know enough about vampires, despite what you've learned through the movies, to know that we rarely care about anyone else but ourselves. Most vampires will lie, cheat, deceive, and murder anyone that stops us from doing what we want. We don't have feelings for anyone beyond ourselves. Sure, we may have what appear to be friends and lovers, but these are people that make us feel good about ourselves, these are people that help us get what we want. When we've achieved our goals, when the person is no longer useful in our existence, they are dispatched. And by dispatched I mean they are let go, eaten, or dripped-dry. You get the picture.

Sociopathic individuals can't care how other people feel. We don't understand your emotions, nor do we want to understand your emotions. We don't care about your overtime, your hours away from your family, or what plans you might have for Saturday morning. Your existence is the service of others, that's what we pay you for. As a vampire manager I have no qualms demanding you work late every evening, no frets over the work that piles up for your weekend, and no second thoughts about calling you on your vacation to ask why you've not responded to my emails. I own you.

When you go to work for a vampire you should expect the worst, it's what you're going to get. I suppose it's not fair that you don't know if you're about to work for a vampire, but you'll know it shortly. Within a few weeks of your tenure under my supervision you'll know that I'm a vampire by my actions, by my demands. I'll demand you to work late, demand that work be redone, demand you to create reports that I might glance over. I may hover just over your shoulder as you do each step of the task. I'm your boss and I'll do as I damn well please. Sure, I may smile, make promises for other days off, but I'm lying. I don't promise unless it suits my best interest.

The Organization doesn't allow me to gouge my fangs into your neck. I'm fed like a pet by The Organization, and since there are rules, policies, and lawyers ready to attack, I have to play nice. I have to act like I'm one of you, though I'm not. I have to pretend to care about the big game, to pretend about the weather, to ask who didn't refill the coffee. Deep down, and you can probably sense this, I'd prefer to murder you and stash your body in my three-drawer filing cabinet. I hate you and want to make your life as miserable as possible.

Excuse me! That was a cheery rant, wasn't it? Once a vampire, always a vampire. It's true that I don't care for you or your suggestions much, but I need you to make business profitable and consequently The Organization profitable. I need you to exist and for that I hate you. So why am I sharing all this with you? Let's just say that I hate some others more than I hate you. Consider yourself lucky – for now.

Why Managers Hate You

If you suspect your manager hates you, you're probably right. Managers, even those that aren't vampires, generally hate you. They don't want to deal with you and your colleagues. They don't want to hear about what problems you're having with your projects, your assignments, or your customers. Managers don't want you to drop by even though the door is open. Managers just want one thing from you: get your work done. Take care of your problems without bothering me. If you screw up, then fix it. If you botch an order, fix it. If you don't know what to do next, figure it out. Managers are busy.

You might think you know what managers do all day, but you don't. Managers have to make certain people, like you and your co-workers, get their assignments completed on time. Managers are reacting to problems within your department, ensuring that the work others do is completed correctly, and overseeing anything that can make the manager look less than perfect. Managers then take all of this information and present it to people higher up in the company, the decision-makers that can change pay, benefits, and determine who'll work for whom. Just as you're accountable to your manager, your manager is accountable to someone else. There's always someone higher up with more and more demands.

That's the general summary of what managers do. Now let's have the honest summation: every manager is different and will be involved in your life to varying degrees of distress. Some managers will hide in their office and let things sort themselves out. Other managers will micromanage every activity to be certain it's done exactly the way they'd like to have it done. Still, some managers trust their staff to do what's best and stay out of the way – unless it's necessary to get involved. Managers, most of them, are people and people act differently from one another.

Vampire managers, however, don't like you and have little problem letting you know how they feel. Vampire managers will demand the impossible, berate you in front of others, and will sacrifice anyone to save their reputation. These things, things like me, don't care about anything but your performance. Vampire managers will do whatever it takes to get you to make them profitable. We are unreasonable, self-centered, and loyal only to those with more power. If you've ever had a manager yell at you, demoralize you, make you look stupid in front of someone else, or just be a mean, mean person, you were probably, and maybe still are, working for a vampire.

Managers have to determine the workload and then predict the utilization of labor to complete the workload. They have to predict not only how they'll keep their staff busy, but also the cost of the staff in ratio to the profits the workers will bring. Managers often get paid bonuses on how well their departments perform – that's why they have no problem piling on the work for you. The more you work at one hundred percent utilization, that is all of the time, the more profitable the department will become. The more profitable the department becomes, the more the manager is likely to earn.

Vampire managers hate you because you can directly affect their income level. If you screw up, then that can directly affect their fancy trip to the Bahamas. If you perform well, and you'd better if you're working for me, you might get a thank you card, a trinket of appreciation, or your team taken out for dinner. You feel appreciated, we feel the paycheck. It's an illusion for management to act like they like you, persuade you to perform well without begging, and all the while hating your guts. That's why they dread to hear about your problems, your issues, and problems in your projects. They just want you, need you really, to do your job.

Motivating the Flesh

The disciple Matthew wrote that the spirit is willing but the flesh is weak. (Don't act surprised, I've read the Bible.) Anyway, Matthew was on track when it comes to the reason why people don't reach their goals, why they let go of ambitions, and why they hate their jobs. People would like to excel to bigger things, have a richer, fuller life, but they lack the motivation to take action to make a difference. For most people it's not just motivation that prevents them from reaching their goals, it's the needed action to get things done. There are lots of reasons why you probably set New Year's resolutions, create goals, and swear to lose weight but you never follow-through. The chief reason, as Matthew said, is that your flesh is weak. It takes mind control over your body. It takes dedication to the cause. And it takes clarity of purpose to achieve anything in this world.

If you were a vampire, and you're probably not, you could take your sweet time to achieve things – because your life wouldn't be disappearing. Your life, however, is slipping on by. You need to take action to achieve your goals and ambitions. You'll be stuck in that sucky job working for something like me for a long, long time if you don't. Sooner or later something will happen in your life: you'll either get busy making changes and taking action or you'll succumb to your fate as another drone filling a role and just getting by.

Think about that: just getting by. There's a management concept. No business would be happy if they just got by, but you're fine with that idea in your life. In business, in the management of you, managers cannot accept the concept of just getting by. Managers expect people to excel, to be productive, and to be profitable. When you work for a vampire you'll be productive enough, profitable enough, or you'll be invited to leave. Your job, my management role, isn't a hobby. People are depending on your ability to achieve and keep your word.

In the olden days motivation was easy: do your job or someone else would. Now it's unions, policies, and lawsuits. Now it is management through lawyers – a wonder anything ever gets accomplished. I mean really, look at your co-workers; how many of them should have been fired a long time ago? How often are they warned while you pick up the slack for them? I appreciate your effort, really, but just think how much more profitable I'd be if everyone just did what they're paid to do.

One motivation theory that is embraced today is based on Herzberg's Theory of Motivation. Fredrick Herzberg was a genius of a psychologist who became one of the biggest influencers on modern business. Herzberg's theory states that there are two types of agents which affect employee performance. First are the hygiene agents that do nothing to promote performance, but their absence will cause performance to suffer and employees to whine and bitch. These are things like a paycheck, insurance, safe working conditions, the lack of neck bites, and other expectations you have when you enter into the employee-employer contract.

The second agent is called a motivating agent and these are the conditions and rewards that promote performance. Motivating agents are the perks that make employees work a little harder – things like bonuses, education, promotions, and responsibilities. Motivating agents can only exist if the hygiene agents exist first. Chances are, unfortunately for management, people won't be real interested in a promotion if they don't get their paycheck. People have expectations that must be met before they're ready to seize motivating agents. As interesting as old Herzberg's concept is, there's a fundamental truth that must be addressed first: the person has to be interested in the motivating agent that's offered. If you're not interested in a promotion, education, or a tiny bonus, you'll not be motivated to do much more than what's required.

The Theory of Motivation is directly related to another management ploy: the Expectancy Theory. This theory states that individuals will behave based on what they believe their behavior will bring them. If people, correctly or incorrectly, believe that their hard work, dedication, and accuracy in performance will bring them a bonus, a pay raise, or continued employment, they'll continue to act accordingly. If the behavior isn't rewarded as promised (or expected) then new expectations are set and people will behave in alignment with the new belief.

The Expectancy Theory also fits nicely with people who work for passive, absent managers. If the worker can be lazy, not complete their assignments, and see other people doing the same without being punished, they'll act accordingly. If these workers are suddenly reprimanded for their performance, their expectations will also be changed and, theoretically, their level of performance will increase.

Working With Exceptional Management

Exceptional management sounds real nice, doesn't it? It's actually pretty ugly. To be accurate it's technically called management by exception. This approach to management means that managers only pay attention to the top ten percent of performers and the bottom ten percent of performers – everyone else is lost in the fray. Management by exception means that management only pays attention to the people who are an exception to the eighty percent in the middle.

It's the classic example of Pareto's Efficiency in Management: eighty percent of management's attention goes to just twenty percent of the workers. The remaining 20% of management's attention is given to golf, web surfing, and bloodletting. Vilfredo Pareto, in case you're one of the curious types, was an Italian economist. He discovered a phenomenon in nature – eighty percent of his pea harvest came from just 20% of his pea plants. I know it sounds like old Vilfredo had too much time on his hands, but it was a startling revelation that applied to the business world, too. For example, a business probably makes 80% of its income from just 20% of its customers. Or, 80% of the office productivity comes from just 20% of the workers.

Management by exception is a favorite ploy of the modern vampire. It's easy to do, keeps people guessing, and allows the middle chunk of the workforce to go wildly ignored. This approach creates competition among the staff to either be top performers or middle performers. You know you've been subjected to this approach when every week there is praise for the same workers and a rotation of reprimands for the employees who aren't meeting objectives.

Another trait of management by exception, and a favorite trick to keep workers jealous, depressed, and disappointed in the office, are zero-sum awards. This award means that everyone else has to lose so that just one person can win. Do you have an employee of the month program? That's a zero-sum award. Everyone's contributions are minimized in comparison to the employee of the month. Now there's some jealousy among the staff and the hatred and envy is aimed at the winner of the award instead of the vampire manager. I especially like to choose the individual that would normally be third or fourth in line to win the actual award to make that person feel awful that more competent workers didn't win. It's evil and I love it.

Some younger managers might think management by exception is a swift way to take care of problems, reward high performers, and create internal competition among the staff. Sure, that's true on paper and in some lofty, MBA-type classes, but it just doesn't work for real management. Management by exception isn't an effective approach to get people like you to be more productive.

Remember, it's about money, not your feelings. Basically, you only matter to management when you're productive. Coffee breaks and long lunches don't earn them more money. When a manager is using management by exception, they're cheating themselves because there's 80% in the middle that's not as productive as they could be. That's a big chunk of profit left on the table; these middle dwellers need to be prodded to do more, create more, and work harder. Management should demand zero defects and 100% quality. While the employees may not be able to reach that lofty goal, at least they'll get closer and closer to doing what's expected of them. Or else.

Your Job Sucks Because of Management

Managers aren't your friends. Managers exist to ensure that you're doing your job. Modern business philosophers may call these folks coaches, supervisors, or team leaders. Whatever terminology is associated with them, you should know that it doesn't change what they're supposed to do: make you work. Good managers, the few that exist, are direct, fair, and tell you exactly what needs to be done and then they let you go do it. If you've a manager like that then there's not much reason for you to read on. Thank god and pray I never come to your company — or you to mine.

When managers blur the line between who's in charge and who's the subordinate, they risk the chance of making poor decisions. Managers do this by allowing team leaders, contract employees, and business analysts make decisions. Managers shouldn't, but do, play favorites – they often can't help it because they're human. If you're cute, handsome, went to the same frat parties, or play golf, you're on the fast track to being liked by the manager. Sure, getting along with the boss has its advantages while it lasts, but then you're the golden child in the office that everyone despises, even if you don't think it's true. The best relationship you can have with your manager is to respect the employee-employer relationship. Show up, do your work, and keep your mouth shut.

Vampire managers, however, aren't that easy to get along with. You can do what's expected of you and that still won't be good enough. Don't you see? There never is a "good enough." You could complete a project months in advance and thousands of dollars under budget and vampire managers would give you grief for providing poor estimates. You'd also set some lofty expectations for all other projects that fall under your umbrella – nice going, champ. We don't care how hard you work, how long you stay at the office, or how much email you answer on vacation – just as long as you do it all, all of the time.

The responsibility of a vampire manager is to make demands. We make demands that will cause you and your colleagues to work late, to do the impossible, to be as profitable as possible. My demands, often in irate and curt emails, rob you of aspirations, rob you of time to look for better employment, and keep you afraid of what we might do to you. There are lots of talented people out there that would love your paycheck, so it's late nights and tough weekends for you. Fear is Chief Operating Officer and you're our favorite employee. Do what we say, when we say it, and without errors, complaints, or pushback. We're pleasant aren't we?

Fortunately for you, I'm going to tell you some secrets. First, you have to do something about the situation or just endure the misery. If you don't speak up, if you don't stand up for yourself, a vampire manager will just keep on demanding, expecting, and controlling your life. You may love the idea of your job, but a vampire manager can make your career and your life miserable.

The best thing you can do, assuming you want to stay in your current employment, is to quit being afraid. Respect is needed, fear is not. Document what the manager wants you to do and then share the documentation with the manager. This will drive them insane. They will wonder how you dare to document what they've asked you to do. By putting their demands in writing and then sharing the demand with them you're getting them to agree to what they've asked you to do. You can get creative and fire off an email just to confirm what they want you to do. There's something magical about putting a request in writing to prevent planned and expected changes, misunderstandings, and additional demands.

Next, do the work that's been asked of you. Do exactly what they've requested, accurately, and record your time to complete the assignment. Now you've a record of what was requested, how long the assignment took, and you'll be creating a record of what you're actually doing for the manager. Be certain to share your time invested and the outcome of the assignment with the manager. When there's a question of your dedication to the employment, you've a history of your contributions.

You do have two alternatives to the documentation and doing the management demands. First, you can continue to do the work as you are now. Whimper and moan, be miserable, and work your life away – that makes me happy. Second, you can quit as quickly as possible. If you don't like your current job and you don't think things are going to change prep your resume and start looking. So basically, you'll deal with the problem or you will not. Of course, there's always the chance you'll just land at a new job working for a new vampire manager. I prefer that you don't, but I'm here to help you move on with your life – before I take it.

Vampires Know Best

There are few things that vampires love in this world. I'm talking about love beyond the obvious – the things and conditions that can make us happy. I might long for a nice, medium rare steak, a good bottle of red wine, and then a fat, black cigar, but it won't do much for me. I've tried and the whole experience was like putting styrofoam in my mouth. I can pretend to get excited about sports, or show an interest in the arts, but these are just distractions from the one thing that really excites me at all anymore: power.

Vampires love power. We love to be in charge, to make decisions, to see the results of what we thought to be true actually come true. We love to show the world that we've achieved something, that we're smarter than others, and that we have a semblance of a life by what we accomplish. Because of The Organization and the way vampires are managed by more powerful vampires, all of our efforts now go into the capitalistic model of earning profits. To earn we have to perform and this means getting people to do the work the way that we want it done.

Management is the collective, unified agreement to direct and control the workforce to bring about a specific result. Management is easy when you have a competent work force, but people are never competent enough. When everyone on the project team knows exactly what they're to do within the project and how to complete their assignments in coordination with other project team members, the project work will practically run itself. That's easy, but what that manager is missing, besides the fun of power, is that the project can probably be more efficient, be completed faster, and become more profitable.

I need the most competent people that my department can afford and I need them to work just as hard, just as dedicated, and just as focused as I do. Okay, that's not true; I need them to work harder, more focused, and more dedicated than I do. I'm in charge and my underlings must respect my commands. They must do the work quickly and accurately (though there's little doubt that I could do the work faster and better). To ensure that the work is done properly I, and other vampire managers, must often supervise each step of the activity in order to ensure quality. We don't have time to do the work twice so it's often easier to just watch the work being done and correct mistakes as they happen. And when it comes to people like you, we know mistakes are going to happen.

Vampires Need Power

Now you've learned something new about vampires: we don't just want power, we need power. It's primal with us, not just a need to perfect the work, to be profitable, but we need to be in charge. We feast on more than just blood; we feast on the control of others. We're smarter, faster, and more productive than you'll ever be so it's natural that we're going to be in charge. What can you do about it? Not much, other than leave and go work for someone weaker, less profitable, and more like you, though how would you know until it's too late? You just might end up working for a vampire that's more of a control freak than me.

Earlier I shared with you Maslow's (less than thrilling) Theory of Needs. You probably got that one in a basic psychology course. Good for you. Have you heard of McClelland's Theory of Needs? It's the same concept, but with fewer parts so it ought to be easier for you to remember. McClelland's Theory of Needs is sometimes simplified and just called the Three Needs Theory because, surprise, there are just three needs that we all have, and there's always one need that trumps the other two. Over time your primary need may change based on your experiences; I know mine has. You can take a proctored thematic apperception test, which is a test based on stories, to determine your needs, but you probably already have a good idea what need drives your actions in your life. Let me share:

The first need is the need for affiliation. People have a driving need for social interaction, friends, and to be liked by others. You can see this need in action with the office flirt, the wiseass that always has something smart to say in meetings, and the social leader for any party or outing. These people, not vampires, have a need for others to like them and they're generally interested in the well-being of others. Good for them. I can use this need to make them lead team meetings, coordinate communications, and deal with people that I don't want to manage.

The second need is the need for achievement. People are ambitious and want to conquer their goals, their objectives. You can recognize this need by the people that are trying to climb the corporate ladder by taking on the meaty projects, pursuing the latest professional certifications, and returning to school for MBAs and other degrees. These people get a charge out of bolstering their resume and adding initials behind their name. I can admire this need, but it's still not for me. People with this need are easy to manipulate: I just assign them the toughest projects, promise educational opportunities, and create impossible objectives for them to conquer.

The third and final need, the need I'm cursed with, is the need for power. There are two types of power that you and I may need: personal power and organizational power. Organizational power is evident with the people that are in love with titles and have a little control over other people in the office. These employees want to be managers, directors, team leaders – anything that gives them the ability to tell others what to do. Personal power is the need to have authority over people not just in the office, but in all areas of life. Go ahead, think of police officers and politicians, but it might also be your big brother or step dad.

By understanding these needs you can identify what motivates people, and for a vampire manager, I can understand how better to control the people that work for me. As an employee you can use these needs to help you in your career. By understanding what motivates your manager, assuming you're not working for a vampire, you can adjust your work habits, conversations, and interactions to appease the need of the person that directly affects your life. If you're working for a vampire manager, they'll have the need for power. If you want to fight against the power, you'll be crushed, but if you go with the power, appease the need for power, defer decision to your manager, you'll likely be more appreciated. I make no promises, but I know it works for me.

Controlling Your Breath and Everything Else

If you've ever meditated, one of the fundamental approaches is to first control your breath. You listen to the easy rhythm of breath in, breath out. It's a relaxing approach to let go of your worries and to just focus on being in the now. I'm not ashamed to admit that I use this approach from time to time – especially when I want to go into a violent rage and let my tendencies, my nature, surge through my veins and kill everyone in the office. Controlling your breath is one of the first approaches to controlling yourself – and when you control yourself, you're more in charge.

Control, however, is something that I just can't have in my office unless I'm the one doing the controlling. Don't you get it? If you can control yourself, then you're controlling your thoughts, your doubts, your emotions, and that robs the vampire of his immediate power. I need you slightly unstable, slightly worried about your employment, and greatly concerned over what assignment I'll demand from you next. I need you in my control, not you in your control. When I keep you worried, keep you focused on my demands, I have the power to manipulate and get you to do what I want you to do. I know you don't like that much, probably resent me for it, but that's how the powerful work.

Much of management is really about staying within defined boundaries and constraints. For example, I have a financial boundary that I must adhere to. There's also a schedule boundary, and there are certainly management expectations of my department's performance that constrain me. This is control from the things above me within the company, within your business enterprise. This is someone with more power telling me what to do – something I don't like very much. I want to be the person, the creature, that tells everyone what to do, but that's just not how it works. So when I have to follow orders I get unhappy, and when I'm unhappy you're going to be unhappy, too. I'll control you because I'm being controlled.

For a vampire, control is such an ugly and beautiful word. It's ugly when others are controlling me, but beautiful when I'm doing the controlling. Just think of the areas that I exert my control as a manager. Within my department I'm always looking for opportunities to control what you do: change control in requirements, cost control, schedule control, risk control, contract control, and my favorite, quality control. Quality control is supposed to be the inspection of the work before the customer sees the work, but it's a fine excuse to poke around and criticize everything you've done.

Everyone talks about quality in the business world, but most don't even know what quality is. Allow me to educate you and the world; quality is not perfection, quality is not the highest level of goodness, quality is not a superior product, service, or condition. Quality is the adherence to what the customer has asked for in relation to the price the customer is willing to pay. For example, if you were willing to pay ten dollars for a meal at a restaurant you'd have some expectations about that meal: a hamburger, fries, and maybe a beer. You can have a quality meal for that price, but if that same meal were to cost $80 you might suspect you're being robbed. Quality is the exact delivery of the requirements, nothing more and nothing less, for what the customer wants to pay.

Let's examine it from another perspective. I have designed my own casket: solid oak, locks from the inside, soundproof, air conditioned, has a great television and sound system, and it's lined with goose down. It's the most luxurious place to spend eternity. When I hired the company to build this for me I gave them the exact specifications of what I wanted. To achieve quality they had to create exactly what I asked for. Imagine my horror when they added a foot massager, a mirror, and a cigarette lighter. This was more than what was required and they wrecked the quality of what I wanted and designed. Needless to say they had to fix their additions and then I fixed them. Permanently.

My point being, vampires need power and control is how we get it. When things are out of our control we may go into denial, make impossible demands, and hold you accountable for what we can't have. I don't do well when I can't have what I want when I want it. All of the management controls are just methods for us to keep our power. If you don't like being controlled, don't work for a vampire.

Vampire Allies: Fear and Doubt

There are two elements which keep you from doing just about anything and they are a vampire's biggest tools to control you. These two elements are fear and doubt. With fear and doubt I can control most everything you do. With just a shadow of fear or a whisper of doubt, you're paralyzed from leaving and I win again. Fear and doubt keep you from taking risks, from reaching your potential, and from ever leaving my control over you. By keeping you afraid of the unknown, by being the unknown, you can't go on to better opportunities.

You may be tempted to start your own business, become a contractor, or follow those early aspirations you've pushed down. But you don't. You doubt your abilities to be successful. You read about the number of business that fail each year. You hear the unemployment statistics and how hard it is to win new business and to actually get paid when you do the work. Your friends and family help with your doubt – though their seeds of doubt are masked in concern and care for your well-being. They'll ask about insurance, about taxes, about your ability to sell and do your services. They'll instill enough doubt for me that I rarely have to do anything. You can listen to these people, but use caution – they're likely suffering under their own vampire managers.

Fear, the parent of career stagnation, makes you risk adverse and keeps you in my powers. You fear the chance of not having enough money to pay your bills, or fear not following government regulations, or fear what your family and friends might say and think if you took the chance to do something great. You probably have the fear of what others may think of your action and what it could mean for your life: you'll be burning bridges, throwing away good opportunities, or wasting your money, talent, and opportunity to do something that probably won't work anyway.

If you're like most people, you talk about someday opening your own business, or writing your book, or trying some acting classes, but you never do. Why? Because you're scared to actually move. That's one of the powers a vampire has – I can paralyze prey with fear and keep them doing what I want them to do. If I see a glimmer of hope, a glint of bravery, or sense you're working towards something that doesn't directly benefit me, I'll start sowing seeds of fear and doubt. It's easy. I'll talk about the possibility of no pay raises, gossip with just the right people about re-organization, ask folks to define their job descriptions. And then you're frantic and your aspirations are tucked away once again.

Fear and doubt keep so many people from ever leaving what they believe is a sure thing to pursue something they'd really enjoy and be good at. You surely know that there is no sure thing. Your job could end tomorrow morning or even sooner. You could die tonight before midnight. You could work for years and years and keep your plans for retirement, but then you're too tired. There are thousands, if not millions, of threatening reasons why you won't follow your heart's desire – I'm just one of them.

When you create fears for yourself, when you doubt yourself, you're really just being weak. You're giving yourself permission to not try, to surrender to the poor image, the poor self-esteem. Do you see vampires whining about what they want? No. We just go do it, take it, and control it. I'm not saying you need to be a vampire, believe me, you don't. I'm saying that you need to exert more control over your life. Believe in yourself, take a chance to make things better, or it'll all be too late if you wait much longer. I know. I may live forever or close to it, but I'll always regret the things I could have done when I had the chance. I'll always regret the opportunities I let fear and doubt scare me from seizing, but that was all before I was a vampire.

Your Job Sucks Because You Permit Control

In business and in your life there needs to be control. Can you imagine the unproductive, unprofitable mess that businesses would be in if it weren't for ample control? If you examine a business without control you'll find waste, unhappiness, and a business that's probably on the way to bankruptcy. Control is needed to ensure that requirements are being met, that customers keep coming back, and that people are completing their work obligations. This control, and my life for it, is why vampires make such great managers. We love the power and control that comes with our job. We love to tell you what to do and demand it be done the way we want.

In your life you need control, too. You can't stay out until the witching hour, squeeze in a few hours of sleep, and then amble into my office expecting to be productive. Your energy and efficiency will be zapped. Control is needed in what you feed your body, how you spend your money, and where you invest your time. I see too many employees sell their day to me and then give their nights to television, booze, and lazing on the sofa. Control where you spend your time and you'll have more time to do what you want. Control the junk that you put in your body and mind and both will last longer.

You have power over your life, something I am envious of. If you wanted, you could quit your job, launch a new business, or return to school, and follow your passions. You could if you really wanted to, if you could conquer fear and doubt, and be pragmatic about your finances, your personal wants and needs, and exert control over your life. Chances are you won't be doing anything differently, one of the things I am counting on as a vampire manager, but you could if you wanted to. You have the power to make decisions and choices.

Decisions and choices are not the same thing. Decisions are a mindset, a determination to accomplish something. You might decide to lose weight, to quit smoking, to find a new job. Decisions are the determination of what you *must* do based on your logic and reasoning. Choices are things that you *want* to do and are based on emotions. You may choose to lose weight because you're emotionally attached to the vision of not being a fatty any longer. You may choose to give up smoking because you realize you're slowly killing yourself. You choose to launch your own business because you're excited about the possibility of success and controlling your life.

See the difference? Decisions are made with your brain and choices are made with your heart. They are both powerful actions, but choices are more likely to happen because you are emotionally charged to accomplish the task. Consider this math puzzle: Six bats are hanging in a cave and two of them decide to leave. How many bats are left? If you said four you're so wrong. All six bats are still hanging there. Just because a decision is made doesn't mean anything has changed. Until we know the bats have acted on their decision and flown away, the decision itself is meaningless.

What decisions have you made? What choices are you pondering? What actions will you take to begin the process to take control and ownership over your life? Vampire managers don't want you to do anything new – at least not anything that negatively affects their control, their profitability, and their dominion. They want you, if you're productive, to keep on being miserable and within their control. Decisions and choices rob them of their control over you and allow you to be free. Of course, once you're gone the vampire manager may just sigh and bring in the next servant to take your place.

If you're pondering, scheming, planning changes in your life – and I bet you are – I encourage you to keep your mouth shut. If word gets out about what you are considering, such as a new business venture, a leave from your present employment, or a new opportunity you've discovered, vampire managers will find out. We have people that want to be us, remember? We have people that will secretly tell us what's happening. In your life, people love to have secrets about you so they can share, gossip, or foil your plans. Keep your choices and decisions to yourself until it's time to act upon them.

By keeping your mouth shut you not only keep the vampire manager from discovering your confidence, you also keep fear and doubt from invading. If your colleagues and manager don't know what you're conspiring to do, then they are less likely to attack your aspirations. It's so tempting, I recall, to share with others what's on your brain, but once the news spills out of your mouth, even if it's just folly for now, there's no going back. You've not only opened Pandora's box of fear and doubt, you've likely raised the ire of a vampire. You don't want vampires breathing down your neck – it's too tempting for us not to bite.

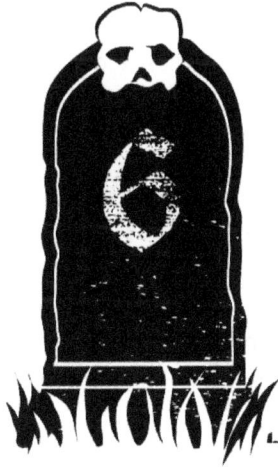

Blood From Stones

I imagine you don't like your job, but are merely tolerating your job. What about your employment before this job? And the employment before? And before? Was there ever a job you really enjoyed? For me, it was working as the night security guard in a publishing company. I sat at a desk until ten or eleven at night and then I could roam the basement halls and alleys around the building undisturbed. No one bothered me and if they did it was the last thing they did. I was free to read whatever I wanted, ponder my life, and experiment with my powers.

That security guard job wasn't demanding at all. I was free to do what I wanted as I saw fit. The sun didn't affect me, I was fine being alone, and there was rarely trouble or incidents. The job didn't pay much, just a few dollars above minimum wage, but it was enough for me to get by on and, fortunately, my simple life didn't demand much. When you have simple needs, no bills, and little care for money, life is much easier. Well, at least that's how I recall it.

I imagine there was a time in your life when you didn't have a pile of bills, the monthly service fees, and all the toys you own. Maybe that was while you were in college or just after school when things were simple and your worries were simple like making the rent, beer money, and Sunday football. When your life is simple it's easier to be happy because there are less worries, less stress, and less vampires to deal with.

And then what happens? You grow older, you begin to want things, you get married, have babies, and then you're an adult with debt and a paycheck that doesn't seem to stretch for the entire month. So you need more income and you do whatever it takes to earn to spend more. And your bills grow and you need more income. And each time you earn more your bills magically seem to grow to fit what you're earning. There's never enough, it seems, so you're constantly looking for the guaranteed paycheck that'll give you the nicer things, provide the more luxurious life, and keep you and your family fed, safe, and comfortable.

There is nothing wrong with wanting to provide for yourself and your family. Everyone wants to be comfortable, to afford nice things, and to have plenty of income to have an illusion of security. Greed, envy, and a desire for more and more and more is a shift from providing a life to you becoming a servant to your paycheck. When you grow to expect and demand a certain lifestyle, it becomes increasingly difficult to break free of the pay in exchange for what may be an uncertain future. And that's what vampire managers love – you not being able to afford to quit. This conversation isn't about debt, it's about being accustomed to your life.

The Lust of Money

When you want what others have, you're coveting. When you want to achieve better for yourself, you're setting goals. What's the difference? To covet means you're envious of what someone has in their possession, their lifestyle, their spouse, their family, their life. When you covet you don't consider the hard work the other person has put into earning what they have. You and others may argue, however, that these people were given monies by their parents, inherited their fortunes from rich uncles, or won the lottery. Well, sniffles.

Life isn't fair. Others will always have more than you, be wealthier than you, and have a lifestyle that's different than yours. This doesn't mean they are happier than you. They may be struggling to keep up appearances, worrying over taxes, fretting over an unfaithful spouse, or fighting a potentially life-threatening sickness. You don't know everything that others have, but it's human to covet perception. To covet is to envy the fruit of someone's hard work. Most people that have nice things, appear happy and appear to have the perfect life have worked hard to achieve those things. You, too, can have those things if you want to pay the price. Nice homes and fancy vacations are expensive and they cost much, and I don't mean just dollars and Euros.

To have employment that pays a significant amount of money usually comes with a significant amount of time invested. Big paychecks don't happen immediately out of school and they often require more than the average nine-to-five commitment. First, there is the educational requirement that's been invested. Doctors, lawyers, even managers have invested years of their life to studying and learning – and there's often massive student loan payments before the rewards come. Next, there's the lowly work, the weird hours, and the demands from their employers – because these professionals are the new hires, just like when you were the new hire. It's no mystery, I hope, that everyone must pay their physical dues, their financial dues, and invest a large chunk of their life before realizing the financial rewards.

In my office I often use contractors to help with certain projects. These contractors bill at a much higher rate than my full-time employees, usually above $100 per hour for their time. Some of my employees have discovered this and there've made comments, whispered snide remarks, and shared their jealousy. What these rubes don't realize, however, is the contractors may earn more, but they also have to pay for their health insurance, their benefits, and all of their taxes. And, for most of these people, if they don't have an assignment they won't be earning anything. The grass isn't always greener over the newest grave plot.

My point isn't subtle: before you envy what others have, consider the price they've paid for their lifestyle. You can have those things too if you're willing to pay the price. Consider the whole picture before you let envy wreck your thought process. What appears wonderful can actually be a terrifying exhausting nightmare when you're in the middle of it. I know many wealthy people who have to work so much they don't see their family, or don't have a family, and certainly don't have time to enjoy their wealth because of the work demands their employers and clients heap upon them.

Miscalculating Risk and Reward

Do you gamble? I have, but the thrill just isn't there for me much anymore. When you gamble, regardless of the game of chance you choose, there's a fundamental rule: never bet more than you're willing to lose. For example, would you be comfortable wagering $500 on a single hand of blackjack? Or would you be more at ease wagering $5 per hand? That uncomfortable tingle you feel with the potential loss of the monies you wager is just one example of your tolerance for risk. If you're like most people, you'd probably feel uncomfortable with the thought of losing $500 in a single hand of blackjack, so you're more comfortable with the $5 wager.

When you're risking more, like the $500, you're also experiencing a chance to win more. It's not tricky; the more you wager the more you could win. For whatever you risk there should be a comparable reward. Most people consider risk in any form to be a bad thing; they're wrong. Risk isn't really all that bad – it's the outcome of the risk, the loss of the time, money, energy, and emotions, that's often painful. When you risk something there should be a corresponding value for the risk. That's risk and reward.

You do this already if you invest in stocks. Your monies could all be lost or you could earn millions compared to what you invested; it's still gambling, but with less probability of loss. When you gamble, or invest, there are probabilities of negative events, such as losing money, and there are probabilities of positive events, such as making money. The earning and loss is the impact of the risk event. If you were to invest a large amount of funds in a startup company, most would consider it a high risk that you'd lose your investment. But, wonder of wonders, if that startup company exploded and the stocks you purchased skyrocketed, you'd be a genius – a rich genius. The risk may have been high in the new company, but the reward was equally as high.

This axiom of risk and reward is true in all that you do. Want to ride a motorcycle? There's risk and reward. Want to open your own business? Risk and reward. Want to keep on working for a vampire? Risk and reward. Look at any choice, any opportunity, and you'll find a corresponding risk and reward. Some people foolishly believe that they're playing it safe by having a job, a career. They think the risk is low because there's security in what they do. My tasty friends, there is no such thing as security; it's a trick to keep you content, earning for me, and to keep your mind from imploding.

Your job could vanish tomorrow. The economy could collapse and the world could burn. Anything could happen. Sure, sure, there's a lower risk of not starving when you're employed by an organization rather than in your own company – but the financial rewards of sticking with the organization are lower, too. When you take the chance to open your own business, become a consultant, or become a professional blackjack player you risk the chance of losing it all or winning big on your investment.

There's another risk and reward trade-off you should consider, especially in the context of your job sucking. When you take the seemingly low risk decision to work for someone else for the security of a paycheck, even a nice paycheck, you also risk the chance of being miserable by not completing your purpose – this additional risk may diminish your expected reward. When you decide to work for someone like me, to earn more and more through your career, meanwhile starving off the thoughts of what you believe you should really be doing, the risk impact is that you'll be miserable.

Thousands falsely believe they're playing it safe by working for a large company that's secure instead of following their passions. These are the folks that aren't even comfortable at the $5 blackjack table - they watch from the ropes. You might earn a nice paycheck, have a beautiful house, and a wonderful family life, but in the shadows of your heart and the sunlight of your dreams there's a purpose crying for you to come to it. Your love is out there, waiting for you, but you've sold it away for something certain, something with low risk and low reward.

Not for Love or Money

When you take a job just for the money you're making a big mistake. Taking a job just for the money will usually guarantee lots of turmoil. In the short-term you may be able to suppress that guilty feeling you have, but in the long run, you'll grow to despise where you are and what you're doing. Yes, it's important to earn a living, but it's also important to be true to yourself. When the only thing that interests you about a job is the salary, you're on the road to despair.

When you work eight hours a day, that is, when you sell your life away eight hours at a time, it doesn't leave much time to do much else. There's the commute to work, and you need your sleep, and then what? You've family obligations, some time to rest and relax, and then your day is gone. That doesn't leave much time for pursuing your dream, your passions. You might be able to give your passion and calling a few hours throughout the week, but your passion demands more than a few hours – it needs your whole life.

When you are doing something that you don't enjoy you'll start to hate not only the job you're in, but you'll begin to hate everything. Your nights will be restless because you know what you've got to do in the morning: go to the job you hate. You'll be tired because you've not slept and the workload will grind on your nerves. Your weekends will be hard to enjoy because you'll be counting down the hours until you're financially forced back to the voluntary prison. Sunday will become the worst day because you know that your reprieve from hell is over and in just a few hours you'll be back to the place that owns your life.

With that cycle of misery you can easily see how your life will begin to erode. Your life will be a long string of miserable days only highlighted by the paycheck. Time away from the office will be full of dread of returning to the office. Eventually you'll become numb to the calling of your life and you'll feel that you're never going to escape the hole you've put yourself into. You'll feel like you're trapped and there's no way out because you've become accustomed to the money the vampires give you in exchange for your work, your misery, and neglect of what you really love.

Money will become your new, yet slightly less attractive, muse. You'll learn to ignore those dreams where your muse is waiting for you, calling for your time, calling for your life, and crying over why you're letting her go. She'll wonder what she has done to you and why you're neglecting her. "Don't you know," she'll sob, "I was ready to give you everything that would make you happy? I was ready to be everything for you. I was why you were born." Those dreams will simply go fade to black and your sleep will become void of dreams. This bleakness is what lies ahead for you, unless you do something about it.

Your Job Sucks Because of Money

Some people feel they aren't making enough money for the tasks they're required to do at their job. Other people feel they are making plenty, but still are unhappy because they too feel they deserve more. Both people have a common problem: they are focused on the money they are paid rather than what they are doing in their life. When the focus of your life is on money and what you don't have, it's impossible to see the things that you do have.

Pretend for just a moment that all of your bills are paid, you have a moderate home, a decent used car, and enough cash to live on. It's not a fancy life, you have to eat meals at home nearly all the time, vacations are simple trips to visit with relatives, and you have to make your clothes and shoes last a bit longer. All of your needs, in this hypothetical situation, are taken care of – you have just enough to live, and you and your family are more joyful. Would you still want to do the work you're doing now?

Most people I've asked that question tell me no, of course not! And then they'll add, "but my job pays me enough to live a nice life. I like nice things, my monthly bills are paid for, and I need to save for retirement." I realize that it was just a hypothetical question, but here's the lesson to be learned: if what you're doing with your life is miserable, is it worth missing out on the joy you could be having? You certainly can have a well-paying career and be joyful, these are not mutually exclusive, but I've learned that it's impossible to be joyful in your life when your job is misery.

It's the money that you're emotionally attached to that stabs your joy to death. When people focus on money, it's not really the money they want. They see the money as an avenue to pay for things they owe, purchase things they want, and as a means to a happier life. No one rolls around in their money and loves the actual currency. People love the money because they think the money will bring them happiness. You cannot, as the old cliché goes, buy happiness. Money can ensure a temporary peace of mind, but there'll always be something to worry about. There are things that money cannot fix.

Contentment, joy, bliss – whatever you want to call it, won't come from money. Money can buy you things and conditions that can set the stage to be joyful, but you can't buy joy, love, or peace with money. I'm not disputing the concept that money can make your life easier, but when you hate your job, what's easy about life? Money and the mistake of joy are what many people fall prey to. They purchase a thing that they believe will make them happy – and so there's a period of assumed happiness. And then the joy of having the thing wears off and they're off to purchase something else for that renewed sense of joy. And then the cycle repeats. Maintaining a job you hate doesn't equate to buying things you love. You won't find happiness in a paycheck or in a shopping bag.

What's actually happening in this cycle is something I've seen many times in my life. People aren't happy, but they try to purchase happiness through things. What's actually being experienced is pleasure, not happiness, not joy. Pleasure is so easy to mistake for joy, but you can distinguish pleasure because the thrill wears away. You can purchase pleasure as often as your wallet allows, but it's a dangerous beast – more dangerous even than a vampire.

When you mistake pleasure for joy you'll chase the pleasure over and over. Eventually what happens is that you'll need greater and greater pleasure to feel the original thrill of the experience. You'll need more drugs, more sex, more booze, more thrills, or whatever the thing is that you've experienced that brought you that genesis of delight. It's a deep, spiraling cavern that will keep you lost in the dark, groping for the next buzz, and keep you ensnared in your current job doomed to repeat the cycle forever.

Though I suppose there is a fate worse than repeating the cycle of seeking pleasure and hating your job. The cycle could end altogether. The chase of pleasure can trap your whole life, so that you may lose that job you hate and in turn you lose the money you needed for the pleasure you've been chasing. Without the hated job and the needed pleasure your life becomes even more miserable. Or you can have a pleasure that drives you over the cliff to the abyss: drugs, sex, alcohol, and more. Or your pleasure can chase those people away that do love you the most. You can imagine the other damage that mistaken joy can have on your life.

One of the things I can't have as a vampire is real joy. It's one of the reasons we hate you so much, one of the reasons I'm generally so angry. When I see you waste your life chasing money rather than pursuing genuine joy it angers me to the point of biting your neck and sucking your blood. But I don't; human resources wouldn't like it.

Real joy, I believe, is a combination of three things that you need in your life (and the three things I crave for daily):

- First, you need to occupy your time by doing something that's worthy of your abilities. When you are employed at a job that's beneath you, not in your calling, or you're there just for the paycheck, you won't be happy. A job that you hate is a job that's not worthy of your time.

- Second, you need a goal, an event, a vacation to anticipate and long for. When you have something besides work to look forward to, it makes life worth living, worth staying alive. Vacations, a marathon, a reunion with your family – these are all events that make life exciting and joyful.

- Third, you need someone to love. When you love someone you put their needs before your own, you want them to be happy, and your heart pounds for them. You think of them as you drift off to sleep, meet them in your dreams, and think of them upon first light. Love is a wonderful chemical reaction between two humans and I'm saddened that I'll never experience that feeling again.

Notice that in these three elements money wasn't mentioned? You might need money to live, to be healthy, to have certain things. You do not need money to be joyful. When you're in the employment of a vampire you're selling not your time, but your joy. You're earning despair that infects your entire life with each minute you surrender.

Your Job Ain't Nothing

When you go to dinner with friends, get together with your family, or even meet someone new what's the first thing you talk about? If your first topic of choice is your job and how much you hate it, then you've a problem. Here's a tip that maybe you already know: no one wants to hear about your job and why it's killing you, why it sucks, and why your evil boss is so evil. Sure, your mom and girlfriend might care for you and want to hear about that mean, old guy, but the rest of the world? Not so much.

Do you want to listen to a whiner? No one else does either. When you talk about your job, you're whining about how rough your life is. Boo-hoo. Unless you're out in the sweltering sun digging ditches with a spoon for minimum wage then your job isn't that tough. If you sit on your rump all day in a cozy, air-conditioned office then your job isn't that tough. If you have a desk drawer full of candy and snacks, coffee breaks, and lunch meetings then your job isn't that tough. If you want to know what tough is go mow lawns for a living, or work the graveyard shift at the grocery store, or wait tables – all for far less than what you're earning now.

Think back on the worst job you've ever had. Even if your worst job was your present job, what was so awful about that work experience? For most people it was their colleagues, the circumstances, the conditions they had to deal with in it. In my experience it was not the actual work that was so awful. It was the horrid boss, the co-workers, and the culture of the company I had to deal with. I imagine your worst job ever was when you were a bit younger, your manager hovered over you, criticized everything you did, and didn't trust you to do your work without their constant supervision. You were probably the recipient of public criticisms.

Let's face it: your job isn't that tough, you're just weak. Brutal? Too bad! I'm here to tell you the truth, not to be a cheerleader. You think your job is tough because it's not perfect, not ideal, not your dream occupation. There will always be things that aren't perfect and components of your occupation that you don't like to deal with – that's just part of you being human. Look at me, I'm a vampire and there are things that I have to do that I don't like very much. You don't see me going to cocktail parties and golf outings to moan about how horrible it is that I have to deal with the likes of you. Suck it up. You need to take a long look at yourself; are you really working for a vampire manager or are you just a whiner?

Work Is Not Fun

If work were fun you probably wouldn't get paid to do it. Very few people actually get paid to have fun: athletes, rock stars, actors, and other performers. But don't be fooled – you just see the end result of their hard work, their hours of grueling practices, and natural, unique talent. It's years of patience, years of doing the hard workouts, and scraping by in menial jobs with the hopes that they'll someday realize their dreams. There's no such thing as an overnight success. The stories of the overnight successes are just that: stories. It's fiction that helps sell more tickets, books, and products. It's all marketing to hide the ugly side of success.

The ugly side of success? The ugly side of success is the despair that you may never find your version of success. The fear and doubts that dreams won't come true no matter how hard they try. It's the nightmare of getting old and having to let go of ambition and having to grab the waitress job, the school teacher job, the management job. The ugly side of success is full of demons, monsters, and scary creatures that whisper to the great that they aren't good enough. These are real monsters that you may never meet, but they're under someone's bed, lurking in the shadows, and hiding under the stairs.

When what you do for money starts being fun you're no longer working – you're living. Do you consider your work fun? I doubt it or you wouldn't be reading this book. You probably are one of the millions living for the weekend and a few days of vacation. You see your time away from your job as your life and your work just as something that's there to occupy your time until you get to do what you really want to do. You probably despise me, your manager, and even some of your co-workers. If you feel the dread on Sunday night through Friday afternoon you're a worker. We own you.

Your negative attitude tells me, your manager, that I'm doing something right. I don't want you to be happy because I'm a vampire and I hate you. Other managers, those that aren't like me, don't want you to be happy for a variety of reasons. It could be your tie, the way you laugh, or how you stop by her office with petty questions just to be certain you're seen. Many managers, however, don't want you to be happy because they see your happiness as a threat to their success. Work is, we've been taught forever, a tough, unpleasant place where we go to make an income to get by. It's not supposed to be fun.

When an employee loves his job, enjoys his co-workers, and is generally happy in the workplace, managers often see this as a person who isn't serious about the work, who's not living up to potential, or who's just a reckless person. After all, work is supposed to be serious business – not a place for people to enjoy themselves, make friends, or be happy. As a manager I see you as a cost – and I don't want to pay an employee to be too in love with the work. Work is hard and it should be unpleasant – so workers should be somber and dedicated to the work. As a vampire manager, when you're in love with the work I suspect you're not doing the work properly or efficiently.

The problem with this point of view, I've learned, is that humans are social animals. You need friends, laughter, love, interactions, and give and take to really work together. People need to enjoy their time and what they do with their time. Don't misunderstand me; work is serious, but people don't need to be serious all the time. Work should be, for things like you, fun, enjoyable, and to some extent a social setting. This doesn't means it's a party where you're throwing Frisbees and chugging beer. I mean that it should be okay to enjoy your job, to be happy about what you're doing, and that you and your colleagues are able to work together, have fun, but also get the work done.

I'm afraid that most managers don't see it that way. If you're smiling you must be stealing from the company. If you're having fun you must be doing something that's not a good contribution to the organization's health and well-being. Managers often see you as property and they expect to get their money's worth out of their property. They don't care if you're happy or sad – as long as you are productive. Management, remember, is about getting things done. You are a thing, you are a piece of equipment, you are selling your time, thoughts, and energy. You are not free to smile, to think, to enjoy your work – nothing is free. Management is paying you to get work done, not to enjoy yourself, not to make friends, and certainly not to be happy. Be happy on your own time.

Why the Devil Loves You

There's an old cliché that says idle hands are the devil's workshop. When you're bored, ignore your work, and stay below the management radar, you're not contributing; you're opening your mind, your actions, and your body to the devil. Yes, the devil. He's not some scary, fanged beast – he's actually a handsome, smug salesman – the kind of guy you'd have a scotch with or take home to momma. But make no mistake, the devil wants to own more than your blood – he wants your soul. And, as I've said, when you're bored at work you're flirting with the devil.

When you're bored and restless your mind can easily wander to all the delightful things that have nothing to do with contributing, nothing to do with your paycheck, and rarely much to do with productivity. When your job is so boring that you're sitting around for hours and days watching the clock tick off the minutes, you'll be unhappy, hate your job, hate your peers, hate your manager, and eventually hate your life. Hate is, to the devil and vampires, a lovely little thing. Hate can consume your thoughts and infect your whole body – even if you're putting on the happy face, you know that inside there's hate and disdain for your work and managers. And that's really just deception, isn't it?

It's not just the deception and hate that makes the devil love you – it's the things your mind dwells on. When you've nothing to do you might think about regrets in your life, you might become depressed and feel trapped at work, and you might start flirting with that sexy married colleague. When you're idle your mind is open to temptations, and, since there's nothing else to do, why not act on those temptations? Don't act on every thought that shoots across your brain, just be aware (and beware) the mental fantasies you create when you're bored. Everyone's mind can conjure up wicked thoughts.

Now grasp this: all actions begin with the seed of thought. If you do it, actually do anything good, bad, or stupid, those actions began somewhere in your consciousness with a thought. As the old proverb goes, "As man thinketh in his heart, so is he." If you want to really know what type of a person you are, examine your thoughts. If you're feeling sad and depressed, are you thinking about sad and depressing things? If you're angry, are you dwelling on events that have made you mad? If you're feeling despair are you focusing only on the negative? What you think about will come out in your actions, your life, and in everything you do.

Living Without a Life

At the other extreme of unhappiness is being too busy. Your job may have so many demands, so many expectations of you that you don't have time to think about much more than deadlines and responsibilities. If your days and nights end with thoughts of what work there's still to accomplish, how far you are behind on assignments, and a mental checklist of priorities, you're not idle but your mind has no energy for the rest of your life. Your mind, body, and actions are sold to management. We still own you – and beyond the workday. While the idle mind may be the devil's workshop, I'll take an overly productive body any day.

There's a big difference, however, between being productive and being busy. Productivity happens when you actually produce something with an efficient amount of effort. Busy just means you have a bunch to do. I hate it when people whine about how busy they are. We are all busy. We all have things to achieve. We all have responsibilities. It's just that not all of us feel the need to complain about our lack of time. The truth is we all have the same amount of time – even me. I can't hold the sun back. I can't squeeze a few more hours out of each day.

People that have much to accomplish are usually good at time management. They understand their responsibilities, their commitments, and promises and prioritize what needs to be done and then go do it. People that aren't that essential, maybe people like you, aren't very good at time management because they don't have much to do. It's true. Think about the day before you go on your little vacation. I bet on that day you can get so much work done because you're going to be gone for the next week. But what happens on your first day back from vacation? You take all day to get one simple task completed.

You've just experienced Parkinson's Law. Parkinson's Law is that work expands to fill the time allotted to it. When you've a big pile of work that must be done today you magically find the energy and the willpower to get it done. When you have a week to complete that same amount of work you'll take a week to get it done. If you know a task is likely to take twelve hours to complete, but you pad the time and promise the results in twenty hours, the task will take twenty hours to complete. Here's the lesson: when you can be productive all the time, even with things you don't enjoy, you have more time for the things you do enjoy.

When your whole life, or most of it, is sold to the highest bidder you don't really have a life. You've sold your time, energy, and thoughts, and you're giving more than your share. When you're so busy that you're working every evening, every weekend, and dreaming about work when you aren't there, you don't have a life. You're probably either running from issues in your life that you just don't want to deal with or you don't have anything else in your life to embrace. Either way, I suspect you despise the work you give and the lack of appreciation you receive. You need to let go, unless you're okay giving your soul to The Organization, or nothing's ever going to change.

Creation Leads to Joy

For the most part, no one is completely happy or completely unhappy – there is a balance, a capacity for joy and misery in one body. The amount of joy or misery however, is dependent on factors within each individual, not just in the workplace. There could be circumstances extraneous to your job that affect your ability to be happy, to achieve joy, but as you spend the bulk of your life working it may appear that what you're doing for an income leads to your joy or misery. And since you're being managed by someone you don't really like, the perception is often that your manager is the bully that's making the things in your life miserable. Your bully manager may be a vampire or you may just be depressed. Doesn't really matter – your perception or reality of your job directly affects your attitude towards your work.

But this isn't all management's fault; some of the blame is with the employees, the cattle that are to be managed. When you were just a little thing you had a concept of your work life being something entirely different than what you're experiencing right now. You probably imagined your work as something you'd enjoy – full of excitement, activities focusing on the heart of your career, and time spent with other smart people. If you had a dream to become an architect you probably envisioned your life creating skyscrapers, designing cities, and constructing art where people worked and lived. You probably didn't imagine all of the regulations, permits, legalities, and other actions that aren't at the heart of architecture, but they're required for the safety of others.

The reality is different than what we imagined. The heart of the work, from computer programming to teaching, is often clogged with the necessary evils of profits, business, and government. It's the damn meetings, politics, processes, and procedures that get in the way of doing what you love to do. When you're in meeting after tedious meeting, reporting to bosses that haven't a clue what you're doing, and are forced to work alongside incompetent people it's nearly impossible to achieve the career goals you've set for yourself – and sometimes difficult to even care.

One of the cornerstones of being happy in your job is to identify what you can create and be paid for. The activity of creating is a joyful act. Think of the parts of your job you enjoy and I'll wager that you'll be creating something. Even if you're an accountant, you're creating tax returns and reports. The process of creating is mentally and physically rewarding work. When you create you're using your mind, your body, and your intuition to pour your essence into the thing you're creating. Even if you're a graphic designer, a technology consultant, or a project manager – there's opportunity for creation in all of these activities. It's the creation, for most people, that's the most rewarding. As a vampire, my essence is in the opposite of creation. My joy is in the misery of others, so you can see how vampire managers need to stifle, control, and harness creativity.

If you believe that old book the Bible, you know that God was a creator, The Creator. Yes, there's a God, but that's not my point. God creates. He created the sun, the world, the plants, the animals, and finally he created man and woman. Because God is a creator, and he created men and women in his image, then it stands to reason that you want and need to create. People are happiest when they are creating. You need to create music, art, literature, buildings, software, and the conditions and circumstances of your life. If you're not creating you're probably not happy.

In your job do you get to create? Are you creating something or are you a supervisor, pushing papers around, and wasting your day in meeting after meeting? If your job won't allow you to create it should come as no surprise that you're unhappy. You need to find a method to create — something to create — in your employment if you're going to tough it out. Identify areas of your work that allow you to create and find a way to do more of it. You must create if you want to live, if you want to excel, if you want to be happy.

Vampires generally don't create; we destroy, we are destroyed. We oversee what you do, but do we really create anything? Management might create reports and contribute to training and create programs, processes, and workflows — but is that really creative? No. Management's role in creation is that of a bystander — we see what you and your colleagues create, but we don't create, we don't make anything new. Now you know another reason why managers, vampires or not, are unhappy in their jobs. They don't get to create and you do. It's just another reason why I hate you.

Your Job Sucks Because It's Work

This may be as obvious as working for a vampire, but some people choose to ignore the obvious. Your job sucks because it's work; it's why you get paid to do it. You don't get paid to sit on your ass, watch television, and eat chips. You get paid to do things that are hard, to do the things that require skills, talent, and your brain and brawn. If your job were easy we wouldn't pay you to do it, you'd do it for free. It's the trade of labor – your time, energy, and effort in exchange for money. It's just that simple. No one, at least in most parts of the world, makes you do your work – you can choose how you sell your life.

If you don't like your job, quit. The trouble with that solution isn't the quitting, it's the affect the quitting will have on the rest of your life. The pleasure of lounging all day on the couch doesn't outweigh the pain of having no money, no food, no home and the boredom that will eventually crowd your brain. It's not smart, of course, to just quit your job without an alternate income plan, but don't be paralyzed from making the plan and taking the leap. It's not going to happen by itself. You don't need a job that you can tolerate, you need an occupation that you'll enjoy and earn a paycheck.

One of the primary reasons your job sucks is because your job is too complicated. Whoever made your job complicated is to blame – it might be you or management – but blame is not the solution. Convoluted jobs are evident when there are more meetings, hype, and dialogues about the work than there is time actually doing the work. This doesn't mean that the work doesn't require meetings and time for planning, just that your work probably needs less talking and more doing. You need to simplify your job. Can you take charge of wasteful meetings? Do you really need to attend every meeting? Find out where your real productivity is, where your real creativity is within your work, and you'll find the most meaningful use of your time. And then do everything you can to get more of it.

It's not enough, however, to just make things simple. You also have to let go of despair, to find hope, and to take risks for a better life. "Don't get your hopes up," someone might say to you. To hell with them. Get your hopes up. Try hard and harder. Create goals. If you want to achieve you have to get your hopes up or there's nothing for you to look forward to, for you to desire in your life. You need hope or you'll be stuck in your job, your life, until it's all over and all too late.

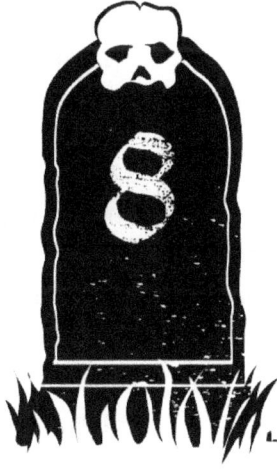

Bored to Death

With some weird people, maybe someone like you, there's an admiration for vampires. Certain people see us as mystical creatures with wonderful powers to read minds, cheat death, and be hip, sexy, and dark. Vampires, I promise, lead a boring life; we can't read minds. Most of us aren't all that cool or sexy, and we certainly can't cheat death forever. Death comes for all of us – just some, like vampires, are on a delayed schedule. It's true that we're smarter than you, have better intuition, and can be mysterious, but that's mainly because we're so considerably older than you. You'd learn how to effectively manage people if you were a few hundred years old.

While the life of a vampire might sound fascinating and exciting, it's not. Back in the olden days when we could do whatever we wanted, my time was just one long adventure. But ever since The

Organization came into being, ever since we created rules, and the shift was made from enjoying our gifts to making money, things got real boring, real fast. Instead of travelling the world, seeing the sights, taking what I wanted, killing what I needed, I only travel now for meetings, all I see is this office, and I'm given what I need and have to purchase what I want. It's now all governance, regulations, and repercussions. All of this structure and organized effort just takes the fun out of being a vampire.

You might think it's great to have the ability to live nearly forever, but forever is a long time. After a hundred years you can get bored easily. I've had friends, vampire friends, that became so bored all they did was feast, lounge on the couch, and watch mindless television. These vampires became pale, their hair greasy and unkempt, and their perfect bodies ballooned with glutton and laziness. Vampires, like people, can get depressed and depression can lead to some ugly things. Some of these friends have simply vanished and others have worked their way out of their funk and are dealing with our new corporate life by making your life a living hell.

I understand your boredom – I've been bored for years and I've got to shake things up a little bit. That's part of the reason I'm sharing this little ditty with you, because I'm bored. Let's talk about your boredom and why you're going to die because of it. There's the death of your ambition, the death of your energy, and the death of dreaming and hoping for something better. If you're persistently bored, it's your soul's way of telling you that you need something different, something better, and something more exciting.

Boredom Bites

When you first started your job you probably weren't bored. The work was new and a challenge to master. But, after time, you perfected the skills needed to do the work and eventually the challenges disappeared and the work became boring, tedious, and sleep-inducing. Work becomes boring when the physical and mental demands are low in comparison to your physical and mental capabilities. You might find your work boring when there's little opportunity for input, creativity, or variation in what's expected. You don't have an opportunity to make decisions – just do the same damn thing over and over in the exact same way.

You might think I'm talking about people who work in manufacturing environments or blue collar workers. Boredom, as you may know, isn't limited to just manual labor. In fact, manual labor can create challenges for exercise, coordination of skills, and thoughts of completing the work with less effort. When you're stuck in a cubicle or hopping from worthless meeting to worthless meeting, your brain can wither like a 50-year-old corpse. Boredom happens when the work isn't challenging and doesn't require much of your capabilities. You're bored when you've mastered a skill and can't find new challenges with the work.

Mastering a skill is good, but allowing yourself to be stuck in the skill as a career is just dumb. Let's pretend that you're a painter that's been hired to paint 1,000 identical hotel rooms. The first hotel room you paint might take an entire day to complete, but by the time you move onto the tenth hotel room you will likely have developed a systematic way of doing the work. You'll create an approach that makes your work easier, makes the actual painting better, and allows you to work efficiently and quickly. You created the system and it's almost exciting to see how quickly you can paint a room compared to the first room you painted.

Now you're onto room one hundred in your painting project. You can completely paint a room in just two-and-a-half hours as opposed to the eight-hour paint jobs when you first started. If you push yourself you can completely paint three rooms in just one day. And then you realize that you're not getting paid anymore by painting the rooms faster. You realize that just because you're more efficient doesn't mean you're more profitable – you still get paid by the hour, not by the level of efficiency you offer. When you first started, the organization was happy with your one-room per day and now they're still happy with two or three rooms a day. You're just a painter, so go paint. And then you have a big management epiphany: just because you're more efficient doesn't mean you have to be more productive.

Efficiency and productivity, you realize, are not the same thing. Efficiency is the system of painting the rooms, the minimum amount of effort needed to create the expected results. Productivity is the actual producing of the results – the quantity of the rooms, the deliverables, the product. While there is a link between efficiency and productivity, they are different. Ideally, the more efficient you are the more you can produce. As a worker, however, unless there's an established rewards and recognition system, there's not much motivation to become more productive. In fact, you may be motivated to be less productive because you're paid by the hour, not by the level of performance you offer.

Now the work that was once exciting and challenging becomes boring and depressing. You realize you've hundreds of hotel rooms to finish and you'll be paid less, because you're hourly, if you work more efficiently. You're punished for being good. There's not a reward for being more efficient. So you slow your efficiency, take longer lunch breaks, or chitchat with your workers as a distraction from the boring work you've mastered. See my point? It's the same in every job where you master the work but aren't rewarded for the mastery.

When efficiency increases without corresponding reward or recognition, you've little motivation to become more productive for a manager that doesn't care. The value of what you do is diminished, the effort to complete the task is minimal, and the surge of boredom is pending. Boredom is bad for you but it's also bad for your organization. Managers often just pile on the work because they assume you can do more, will do more, whether you're bored, capable, or interested.

Repetition may be the mother of learning, but it leads to boredom if you can't move on to more challenging assignments. If you're bored out of your skull at work it's because you don't find the work interesting. This doesn't mean that what you do is necessarily easy. Consider the tedious work of completing a tax form and how boring that, too, can be. Work that's tedious can equate to work that's too boring. We all have different activities that excite us and, unfortunately, work isn't always one of them. Jobs aren't exciting all the time. There are rules, standards, regulations that you have to follow – many of which were created by vampires – and these boundaries create the boring work. Tough for you. The secret is to find work that's enjoyable enough to balance the tasks that you must do, but don't want to do.

Maybe You're Boring

I'm a vampire, so I can be as mean as I want. Think about the work you're doing and why it's boring. Sure, there's the tedious work that's really important, but chances are the work you find boring isn't really all that important. You might be assigned to do the work that no one else wants to do because, well, you aren't all that important. This doesn't mean that you aren't an important person in your lover's life or important to your momma. I'm sure you are. Chances are if you're stuck doing the ugly, boring work it's because you're not that important to your manager.

If you were a manager like me would you let your most valuable asset do the least important work? Nope. The people that are most valuable to me do the most valuable work while the people that aren't my top performers get the ugly, low status jobs – the dirty boring work. Maybe you're lucky and you only have to do the boring work occasionally, not all the time. Good for you, but if you're doing the boring work day-in and day-out then chances are you're not that important to your manager or your organization.

Just because the work is boring doesn't mean that you aren't compensated. You might be getting paid because the work is boring, is tedious, or smelly, or it's the crap job no one else wants to do so it lands on your desk every month, week, or day. Lucky you. When you're stuck with the boring work over and over you probably feel unappreciated, undervalued, and not all that important in your role in your company. Probably those feelings are valid and that's just another reason why your job sucks.

When a person is stuck doing the same old boring tasks there are only a few options that make sense to deal with the sucky work. First, examine the work and see if the work really has to be done – is this work an effective use of your time? If you're billing $100 per hour, it's not a good use of your hourly rate to spend it sweeping out the parking garage. If you recognize an activity that's a wasted use of your time and talent speak to your manager. Tell your manager what you should be doing with your time – and why.

The work you do should be in proportion to the income you're generating. Some would argue that you should do whatever's requested of you regardless of what you're getting paid. This is true to a certain extent – no one should be above manual labor, but as a manager I don't want to pay a top dollar for a resource to do a stupid task that's not really needed. It's more cost effective to move a highly-paid resource to more income appropriate activities and move the low-paid grunts over to these menial duties. Of course, you might already be the low-paid grunt doing the menial work.

The Cost of Boredom

Once you've mastered the task, you can switch from mastery to boredom. Managers sometimes don't consider the cost of boring work. When you're bored at work your attention to detail can slip, injuries can happen, and you just might quit. While no one is irreplaceable there is cost and uncertainty associated with hiring someone else to do what you do so adequately. Labor is almost always the highest cost of an organization.

When employees quit a job because they're bored it might be good for the employee, but it's generally not-so-good for the employer. Now the manager has to find someone else to take your spot, train them how to do your job, and then patiently watch as the new employee grows into, hopefully, the same level of efficiency as you. You may have done the boring work for so long that your level of efficiency is years above the new worker's efficiency and productivity. In other words, your mastery of the task saved your company money – the new guy can't yet (if ever) do it like you did.

Boring work can also be costly from a healthcare perspective. There was a time in the world when you just did your job without all the complaining. If your shoulder hurt, well, that's too bad for you. Eventually your shoulders became big and strong and you got paid to exercise. Or if you lopped off a finger in a factory you bled a bit, learned to work with nine fingers, and kept right on working. Now workers moan about the height of their monitors and the comfort of their chairs. There is some cost-savings to making work less boring by making it less monotonous. Repetitive stress injuries can happen to employees costing thousands in health insurance premiums, loss of labor, paid wages for less productivity, and general unhappiness. It's most cost effective to reduce or eliminate monotonous tasks so that employees can be more productive and ultimately more profitable.

Boring jobs are usually jobs where people have no decision-making responsibilities. A long (and probably overpaid) study at the University of West Florida reports that people with jobs with no decision-making duties were 43 percent more likely to die than people who make lots of decisions every day. The fewer decisions you're required to make, the more likely it is that your job is of low value. Therefore, low value jobs equate to your death. There was a time when this would mean a buffet of meals for a vampire manager; now it just means more professional development, more analysis, and more incentive to keep you working.

This same study reports that men are generally more bored than women. And another non-surprise is that people who are bored at work often engage in riskier behavior, enjoy dangerous activities, and may experiment with drugs and gambling. For a manager that's just more worry, stress, and people we'll have to replace. An organization may have great benefits, decent pay, fun employee break rooms and offerings, but if you're the guy stuck doing the boring work your focus will be on the dull dread of the work and not all the perks the job includes. Stay in that boring job and purchase a hefty life insurance policy.

Your Job Sucks Because It's Boring

If your job sucks because it's boring then you need to do something about you – not your job. I'm making the ghoulish assumption that you don't want to remain in your mind-numbing, life-sucking rut of boredom. I'm assuming you're ready to make some changes to your life to make your job and your career, a bit more interesting than it is now. If that's not you and you're content to keep right on chugging along in your boredom, you're an idiot and I'd be scared to drink your boring blood.

Moving along. You know why your job is boring – because you've mastered your responsibilities, the tasks are monotonous, or the job is tedious, or a thousand other reasons. Knowing why the job is boring is your first approach to solving the problem. Can you change the way the work is being performed? Examine the workflow to determine if there's a more efficient method to get through the boring work faster, with greater accuracy, and ultimately more productivity. If you can control how the work is done then you may find the work itself to be less boring.

If you can't change the work, how the work is done, or the monotony of the work then you need to look for other solutions away from the work. If your current work isn't going to change then you have to change what is your work. You should first look internally within your organization for opportunities that don't involve the boredom. Ask for more responsibilities: train others on the work you've mastered, get involved with team leadership, find problems and create solutions. If you can show management that you're more than just a tedium worker, your value increases and you're more likely to get more responsibilities and less boring work.

You probably won't like this next bit – especially if it's true – but your work may be boring because it's all you qualify to do. If you don't have degrees, certifications, professional training, and years of experience it's difficult for an organization to give you more responsibilities and more important work. This isn't an insult or even a trust issue – it's a risk issue. Think of the roles in an organization that make decisions for others, that aren't seen as boring. If the individuals with these roles aren't effective then it's a costly mistake for the organization. If you don't have the apparent qualifications then it's not worth the risk to the organization to allow you be less bored but more likely to screw things up.

If you want more responsibilities, want a better job, want higher pay, and want exciting things to do then there's really just one common element you need: education. Education is the key to opening the doors of more exciting career. The most obvious form of education is the college education – though you should be certain that the investment in time and money will be in the area of what you want to do, not just where the apparent money is. You can have a college degree and still end up in a boring job because the job isn't what really appeals to your soul. Choose wisely when it comes to your career – it's what you'll be doing for a long time.

Certification classes and self-education are two other choices for proving your expertise. There are live, online, and self-led classes for just about any topic you can imagine. You can choose certifications in technology, management, health care, real estate, and hundreds more. One advantage of your boring job is that you can probably allow your brain to think on other things while you're doing the boring work. Think about what you really want to do, what you really want in your life, and then explore the educational gaps to move from here, where you are bored, to there – where you want your ideal life to be. Quit wasting heartbeats.

You may already have certifications and degrees but have nonetheless found yourself trapped in a job that's too boring. This sure doesn't mean you're done learning; if you think you're done learning then you're probably destined to be a mouth-breathing fleshbag where everything about is you boring. Never give up on learning. Read books, take classes, listen to smart people give lectures, find new challenges. Life, for people like you, is rich with opportunities to take in new things, to grow into a new person.

If your job is boring by design and there are no opportunities for advancement within your company, it's time to look elsewhere for employment. Why stay in a boring job with no challenge, no growth? You need to get your resume polished, network online and in-person, and find a job that will support your needs, wants, and life goals. You don't need to waste any more time in an organization that will kill you slowly with boring, tedious work. Your life is too valuable – I envy it.

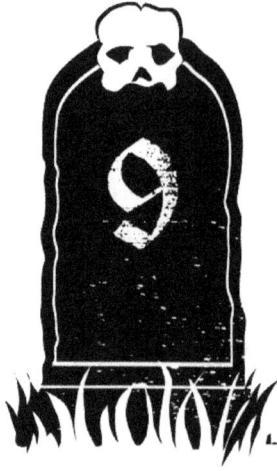

It's the Bloody Business

There are lots of reasons why your job can suck: it's boring, your manager hates you, it's stinky, your co-workers are idiots, and countless more reasons. But all of these reasons for a miserable job pale in comparison to one of the biggest reasons why jobs can suck: the entity you work for, by design, sucks. If the structure you operate within is poorly designed, poorly orchestrated, and poorly communicated then it's no wonder that you'll feel awful. It's no wonder when a third of your life is spent in an incoherent space, with poorly written rules, evil managers, and unspoken politics that you've given up hope.

Large, cumbersome organizations – like hospitals, banks, and insurance companies – are notorious for over-managing their employees. By over-managing, I mean they create rules, policies, standards, and guidelines that have little to do with the success of the organization and even less to do with how well you do your job. If your organization has a rule where you must wear your identification badge, your organization sucks. If you work for a manager that loves to enforce this rule then you're working for a vampire. If your projects and people are in disarray and managers are focused on enforcing childish rules then you're in a world of hurt.

There gets to be a point in an organization's size where the company practically runs itself. People and businesses will still buy and sell with the large company regardless of the rules, the cubicles, the vampires, the bloodletting, and the wretchedness that happens behind closed doors. The quality of service may stay the same for customer expectations and service – but that doesn't mean that the quality of service is exceptional. Rules, reorganizations, seating charts, and policies are only needed if they support the vision of the company – far too many managers, and not necessarily vampire managers, fall in love with power.

It's not just the large organizations that can suck with rules and overly complex structures. It's also the smaller businesses, the mom and pop shops, and the startup companies that can have vampires lurking in conference rooms. Small businesses can be small by design, but they can also be small because the owners love the absolute control, ownership of the work, and the dictatorship they have over the employees. Rather than get out of the way and allow the employees to do their work to make the organization more successful, small business owners can suck the life out of employees' work, creativity, and ambition through criticism, unreasonable demands, and constant hovering.

Vampires in The Organization have had a tremendous, unexpected effect on how businesses operate. In our desire to be more organized, more in control, more profitable, non-vampires have seen what our managers do, the results we've created, and they've emulated our approach. While our goal was to be profitable to get more blood, companies have taken more blood to be more profitable. And you call me the monster.

Working for the Ruling Class

One of the reasons why your job sucks is because you're working for people that used to be hallway monitors. They love to create rules to control what time you show up, when you can have a break, what you can have around your cubed desk, and even what you have to wear to work. Rules are good to an extent – it's good to have a safe, clean, productivity-promoted work environment. No one wants to sit next to a guy that sings along to every country-western song for hours on end. No one wants to sit next to a woman that paints her nails every few hours. There has to be some common, agreeable boundaries to ensure that the workplace is good for all of the employees.

The problem with rules, however, is that when a person creates a new rule and sees the workers actually following the rule there's a surge of power. If your manager creates a rule that you can't have coffee cups on desks there might be some initial outrage, but eventually there'd be no coffee cups on desks. Now the manager sees the power he has over the sheep and he likes it. He decides that everyone must have only black ink pens on their desk. And then there's a rule for no cartoons on the cubicle walls. And then a rule banning cell phones in the office. With each new rule there's a new surge of power, control, and gratification of telling you what to do.

A classic vampirism can be found in your office dress code. If your office still requires men to wear suits and ties and women to wear business suits there's something to be examined. Business suits and ties maybe appropriate if you're working in a stuffy financial environment or a vampire-filled law firm, but if you don't see customers, your customers wear jeans and t-shirts, or you're using more brawns than brains, a tie won't help you do your job better. It's really a shame, in my opinion, that adults need some guidance on what type of clothing is appropriate for work, but some people are just stupid.

Unfortunately for you, it's the stupid people that come to work dressed like they've just returned from a beach vacation that give managers the reason to dress you how they want. It's more control beyond your time in the office. Don't kid yourself, if your office has business casual you're just wearing a uniform with loosely defined rules. If you want to fit into any business casual environment get yourself some khaki pants and a blue shirt – you're part of the masses. You're no longer special, unique, creative – you look and act like everyone else.

Dress codes may keep employees looking professional, keep the paid masses in uniform, and provide some visual structure to the employees, but it's really about control and power. Proof? Do you get to wear jeans on Friday? Do people get excited about the thrill and comfort of wearing some jeans one day a week? It's a sham. Does productivity dip to near zero on Friday because you're wearing jeans? No. It's unintelligent that a company has a dress code Monday through Thursday, but dress codes don't matter on Friday. What you wear generally doesn't affect how productive you are. Management controls more than just your attire if you're excited about jeans on Friday – now they control your emotions. Want some subtle vengeance? Wear a suit and tie on Friday. Take the one day management encourages you to wear something casual and wear the opposite.

While some vampire managers might like to play these games, there's not much profitable benefit to setting rules only to bother you. If the company is as profitable as it's going to get, if the sales numbers are good, if the manager has met or exceeded quotas –

then the vampire manager might torture you with asinine rules for her pleasure. But when the company needs to be more profitable, when the manager's numbers are slipping, and when there's customer chaos, the focus shouldn't be on anything other than becoming more profitable. Idiot managers miss this point — businesses exist to make money, not to control people.

Designed to Control the Masses

In big businesses there's thought and planning that goes into the design of the organization. You have lines of business, departments, functional groups, and other ways of dissecting a company to create boundaries, fiefdoms, and segregated control. Vampires love this because it gives us power over our little chunks of people, keeps us separated from other vampires, and lets us control our people the way we wish. As long as our entity is profitable we can treat you however we want. As long as we follow orders from The Organization we own the things that work for us. We can create the rules, tell you where to sit, and toy with your emotions, sanity, and hopes, to entertain ourselves.

The most common type of organizational structure is a functional structure. This means that your organization is chopped into areas by the types of work each department does: sales, marketing, technology, education, and others. Functional organizations are full of vampires because each functional unit is led by one person — the functional manager, though you may know her as the director, the vice president of whatever, or the unit manager. Doesn't really matter what title you attach to this functional manager, they own you and the resources within your group. Functional structures create internal competition and each department is pitted against the others. If you need some IT help you have to buy it from the IT department.

At the other end of organizational science is the projectized company. This structure creates teams for each type of project work. People are put on a project for the duration of the project and that's all they work on. The project manager is in charge of the project team and he usually reports to a project management office or program manager (which means there are two vampires to deal with). When the project is over the project team goes onto other projects or they mysteriously disappear from the company. Projectized structures are what you might find in new businesses, construction crews, and IT consulting firms. You can expect lots of turnover, but generally happy professionals – because each person knows what's expected of them for the duration of the project. Anxiety increases as the project nears its completion because the project team may wonder what their next assignment will be – or if they'll be released from employment.

The matrix structure is what most larger companies try to emulate. The matrix structure means that the resources that actually do the work exist in each department but are assigned to project managers for special work. The matrix structure allows resources to be used around the organization whenever there's a need. While this looks happy on paper, it is sad if you're a talented, underpaid resource. It's like having blood type O+ in a disaster zone. You're assigned to lots of different projects, jerked from meeting to meeting, and the work continues to pile up. And because there are plenty of vampires to deal with – and vampires play politics with other vampires – you're caught in the middle.

The matrix structure has both functional managers and project managers that assign you the work and demand constant reporting. You can imagine, or maybe you've lived it, that you have to keep the functional manager happy and the project manager happy. Both of these people can make your life hell with just a few assignments, conflicting directives, and neck bites. If the project manager and the functional manager won't communicate with each other then your life becomes more complex as both will have demands that can be mutually exclusive. You'll eventually come to a point where you can't please both managers and one, or both, will be disgusted with your performance.

While the functional, projectized and matrix structures all sounds crisp and clean, few businesses actually map perfectly to any of these structures. Companies are usually more composite in their structure; you might operate like a functional organization, but for a few special projects you're shifted into a matrix environment. Or you might be a matrix structure, but the functional manager is going to lead the project management. Or you might be just a resource on the project, but now you're also serving as the project manager. A composite structure is just managerial talk for describing dysfunctional organizations. Vampires love the confusion – it keeps the focus on you and off of us.

Managing the Hated

Do you really hate your manager? I bet more managers hate their employees than the other way around. As a manager your day is full of constant interruptions, constant questions, constant emails that don't matter. If you're a vampire manager, dealing with people becomes amplified; it takes all of my power to not leap over this desk and finish you off. But I don't – it's against company policy. You can hate the vampire manager – he likely hates you too.

Consider things from the manager's perspective. He probably came up through the ranks to become the manager – he's done your job or something like it so he understands what it takes to get things done. Technology has changed since he actually did the work and he's not had the time (or desire) to keep up. Now technologies are totally different than when he was doing things and there's a sense of disconnect from what you're doing and what he used to do. Yeah, he's scared to look foolish to you because he doesn't understand what you do even though he used to do it.

This evolution of worker drone to manager also has another side effect: no one will ever do the work as good as the manager used to do. Your manager may have been a systems engineer for years and years, but now she's calling the shots and you're doing the work. Only your work isn't nearly as good as she used to do it. You can never, in her mind, do the work nearly as good, nearly as quickly, and certainly never better than she did in her past life. Ego is a dangerous element for managers and it comes out with big fangs and sharp tongue. Vampires with ego, which we have, are thrilled to cut your work down because you just can't do it like we used to. You're an amateur compared to the years of experience and depth of knowledge that we have.

As a profit-driven vampire there's an internal conflict between wanting to make your life hell and making the business, The Organization, profitable. When employees are unhappy, productivity suffers, employee theft increases, and employee turnover skyrockets. Disengaged, unchallenged, spiteful employees can cost The Organization thousands every year. When employees are happy, engaged, and feel valued, then absenteeism decreases, customers feel more connected, and there's less stress for the average manager. For a vampire manager, however, the goal is often to control as much of the employee's life and happiness as possible without affecting the profitability of the company too much. In other words, we want to give you as much pain as possible without affecting the bottom line too drastically.

Managers, good managers, can decrease the hate in the workforce by being smarter about how they hire new employees. First, hire better employees. Like most things in life, you get what you pay for – but paying more doesn't automatically mean better workers. In-depth interviews, proof of experience, and having an experienced professional interview the employee are all needed to make informed decisions about the new hire. Second, train the employee how the job is to be done. I'm not talking about training employees how to do the mechanics of their job, but train them on what's expected of them in their role in the company. Finally, evaluate employees on a regular basis to determine what's working, what's failing, and what you're going to do about it.

Your Job Sucks Because Business Sucks

 Businesses exist to make money, not to give you a job. The focus of a business is on the profitability of the company, not on how happy you are as an employee, what your goals are, and what you want to accomplish in your career. Employees and managers lose focus of this business fundamental. Someone started the company you work in; they took a risk, gambled their money and reputation that they'd make a profit based on an opportunity they identified. Unless you're the business owner you haven't really invested your blood and sweat into your company, your life. You don't know what it's like to lie awake at night wondering and worrying about payroll, new customers, taxes, and keeping a profit margin. You don't know what it's like to fret over working for free while employees take long lunches and donut breaks, and then question you about vacation time.

Business owners and good managers aren't just stressed and anxious over employees, there's also the flood of regulations, forms, licenses, insurance, banks, and other bureaucracies that plague their life. Many employees just show up, do their job and collect their pay. The business owner and managers have to deal with mounds of paperwork, forms, attorneys, accountants, bankers, and other people that don't help the business grow or increase profits.

Imagine the business owner that started a company out of love for the work. The business owner may love the work, but there's also the desire to make a profit and grow the business. As the business grows so too does the management responsibility, the complexity of the business, and the need to hire employees. These necessary evils begin to multiply and while the operations may boom, the owner moves farther and farther away from the love that started the business in the first place. Now there's resentment, spite, and anger towards all of the things that lie between the owner and the original activity that launched the endeavor all those years ago.

Managers settle between the business owner and the employees. The managers feel the turmoil from the owner and so, in turn, the turmoil trickles down to the employees. The employees feel the turmoil and they begin to hate their manager, the manager feels the hate and he begins to hate the owner. It's a vicious cycle that creates animosity throughout the company, distrust among the managers, and a sense of disconnect in the entire organization. Throw a vampire or two into this mess and you'll have a company full of backbiting, snide remarks, bad attitudes, and general depression.

I know I'm painting a grim picture, but it's not that unusual for businesses to grow from something founded on love to something operating in an environment of hate, discourse, and turmoil. The organization you work for may be decades old and the original business owner may be long gone, but the company can still be a horrible place to work. When the focus of the executives and managers is shifted from the original vision and purpose of the company to the structure and mission of profits, the culture of the company changes regardless of whether the original owner remains. Profits and capitalism aren't bad, but when they're the only purpose, the real mission, and the sole intent of a company your job will suck.

I'm a vampire manager in The Organization. There are just three things I really want: profits, blood, and more profits.

The Heart of the Matter

You know I despise you and am jealous of all that you can do that I cannot. As a vampire I have things you don't – powers, intuition, a long life, and control. But you have the things that make you human: the ability to feel, to love, to eat, and to choose what you want with your life. I, too, can make choices, like writing this book, but there will be, could be, deathly consequences for what I've shared. You might be able to play nine holes of golf on a sunny Saturday morning, drink a few beers, and work on your tan. I'll choke down a couple of pints (different beverage than your pints...) and hide in my office because I've nothing better to do.

I do hate you, but not because I hunger for your blood or am envious of your suntan. I hate you because you have the whole world in front of and you gripe that your job sucks. You can decide to do whatever you want, whenever you want – if you want it bad enough. You can make a choice right now to become a painter, to be a writer, to learn how to play a guitar, or you can choose to go right on working in that hellacious job, commiserate with your colleagues, and pine your life away waiting for the mystical, imaginary someday when you think your life's actually going to begin.

Don't you get it? Your job may suck, but your job isn't your whole life. No one, I bet, is holding a gun to your head every morning and ordering you to get to work to an occupation you hate, dread, and cry over. You can pack up your belongings right now and walk out the door never to return. Fear keeps your ass planted in that cushy desk chair though. Your fears may be legitimate: how will I eat, pay the bills, take care of my family, and what will I do next? Your doubts shake your confidence that you could have a better job, start a business, or make a living doing the thing that your heart cries to do. As I mentioned earlier, fear and doubt will keep you where you are, where I and my brothers and sisters can keep eyes on you, keep you down, and hold you hostage for years.

You have to decide what you want of your life. If you do nothing, nothing will happen. Sure, there may be some happy accidents, chance encounters, and good fortune just might fall in your lap. Are you willing to just wait for the possibility of good luck or do you want to take charge, take the initiative and go make things happen in your life. You must choose what you want to do. Not taking an action, such as staying right there in your sucky job, is an action. There is no such thing as doing nothing – by choosing to do nothing you are choosing the prolonged misery, the day-by-day death, of your present circumstances. Do something or endure the misery.

Choosing to Fight

Movies and scary books make you believe that vampires are almighty beings that can put you in a trance, seize your mind, and wrestle you to the ground with our super strength. That's a nice premise for the Hollywood movies, but it's not the reality of the vampire. What we have that you don't are the years of experience; we know what it takes to manipulate, to make you afraid, to whisper the fears of uncertainty, and to get your mind wandering towards the worst-case scenarios. But that's nothing supernatural – it's what most managers know anyway.

So here's an important hypothetical question: if I were behind you and you could feel my breath on your neck, my fangs scraping across your skin, and my cold hands on your shoulders, would you fight? Would you have the courage to push me away, to protect your life, to struggle against certain death? Or would you be like so many others that aren't with us any longer – the people who gave up, who turned the neck and let my fangs sink into their veins and drain their life? Are you a fighter or a quitter? Do you want to fight for your life or give it away?

I suspect you want to fight. I suspect you want to go right on living, enjoying your friends and family, seeking joy, and looking forward to long days of happiness. You want the loving spouse, the happy children, the beautiful life, and the joy of doing meaningful work. You want your life to be abundant with joy, peace, and strong relationships with people you admire. You want your work life to be full of meaningful, valuable work that's not boring, demeaning, or far from your heart's desire. You have a purpose that you've yet to meet and it's your mission to fulfill that void in the world. You have a desire to push me away and fight for what you want.

Having the desire isn't the same as actually fighting, though. There have been plenty of victims who wanted to live on, who wanted to fight back, yet who didn't. Maybe they were too afraid to fight for what they wanted, or they didn't believe they'd have a chance against someone like me, or they didn't think they deserved any better in life. What they didn't realize may be the same mistake you're making: you have to fight for what you want in your life. No one is just going to hand it to you. Do the work, create the life you want, and know that your life is already happening – not at some future someday.

While you and I may never meet, you need to fight for your life. If you hate your job, despise every minute you waste there, and have outgrown the challenges of your work, you need to do something else. Your life is limited and each day you sell is a day you no longer own. You might as well be dead – or nearly dead – when your life is full of things you don't want to do. This is your life – do what you want, what you can, with it. Don't wait until it's too late - being dead lasts a long, long time.

Your first step is to determine what you want to do with your life. Some idiots reading this book will say they want to sit on the beach and drink margaritas all day. Sure, go ahead and do that – just keep out of our way and don't bum for loose change, okay? For the serious, the people that want to contribute and live an extraordinary life you need to decide what you want to do with your time, how you want to contribute, and what talents you're keeping tucked away. Examine the statements you make to friends where you talk about doing such and such someday: opening a bakery, being a writer, going back to school. Someday talks are really your way of floating ideas out there to see what others think about those dreamy aspirations. Don't worry what others think – if your heart is longing to do it, to be it, you should make it happen.

The most important thing you can possess, something that your colleagues and friends probably do not, is the ability to know what you want. That's one of the problems so many people have – they don't know what they want so they choose nothing. It's like when you have hundreds of television channels to choose from so you keep changing the channel hoping for something better than the last. When you're constantly looking for something better and better you often end up with something far, far away from your heart's desire. Narrow your choices to the most valuable things you want to do and then choose one of them. Often, the worst thing you can do is nothing.

It Sucks to Be Stuck

It's possible that your job doesn't really suck, but it's not all that great either. It's just a place you go to earn the money to live. Unfortunately, you might feel that you've been there so long that you're now stuck in that job, in that position, forever. There's only one position you're going to be stuck in forever – horizontal in a casket, six feet under. If you want to change, want to get unstuck, you can. It won't be easy, but you didn't create your work situation in just a few days. In order to get unstuck in your career you'll need to take action and change some elements of your life.

Albert Einstein said, "You can't solve a problem with the same level of thinking that created the problem." You need to change the thinking – and the actions – that got you stuck. It takes a different type of thinking and then acting on the answers to get things moving in the right direction. Look at what's different now than when you first started that job. Consider the original intent and purpose of the job, the actions and lack of actions you've taken to reach this place, and then consider what's different now. Determine what needs and values have evolved and changed in your life since you agreed to the opportunity. Think and act differently and you'll get different results.

Often people are not stuck – they are just afraid. Examine the fears surrounding the goal you're almost ready to pursue and you'll probably find fears that can squelch your energy to move forward. It's human to be afraid. Common fears that prevent success: fear of what others may think of your success, fear of exceeding expectations, and fear of the unknown. Examine the fears surrounding your goals, document the fears, and determine their validity. Create a plan to manage the fears and you'll often find relief to move onward and upwards once again.

It might seem odd for you to hear a vampire talk of meditation, but it's one of the few mental exercises that can make me feel human again. Meditation might seem odd if you've never tried it before. It's simple, really. Find a quiet place in your home, a park, or office and sit still. No phone, no internet, no interruptions; you are not available in this time of silence. In today's world there is too much noise, too much static, and too many electronic distractions. I firmly believe that when things are stuck it's essential to regularly seize time alone and just think on life, how you can use your energy, and what's best for you. Take a small slice of your life and be calm, be still, and be peaceful. You'll often find a solution to your problem and rekindle excitement, passion, and focus to attack the problem.

Managers use an approach to project planning called decomposition. Managers will take the scope of the work and break down the requirements into smaller objectives. Then we'll break these objectives down again and again until it's easy to see the tiny elements that collectively create the scope as a whole. You can, and should, use this same approach in your goal achievement. When you're stuck, examine the problem and decompose the problem to smaller, manageable elements and then create a plan to accomplish each of the smaller pieces of the situation.

Your Job Sucks Because It's the Wrong Job

If your intent is to get a job as an accountant but you really, really want a job as a software developer, you'll never be truly happy in your pursuit of the accountant's job. Your purpose in life should make you happy – not just making money. Examine the goals you have set and determine if these are the correct goals for you or do the goals exist only because other people have imposed them upon you. A goal that you don't really want, aren't excited about, and don't enjoy working toward isn't going to create passion, joy, or excitement in your life. If you don't have the right goal, scrap it and create the goals that thrill and excite you. Or come to my office, bare your neck, and let's get it over with.

If you're in the wrong job, you're keeping yourself from being happy, really living your life, and finding your purpose. You might think you can't afford to quit, won't be able to maintain your current lifestyle in a meaningful job, or that you aren't smart or good enough to do what you really want to do. I'm telling you that you can quit that job and launch your career. Your life is too temporary to shuffle along in a job you don't enjoy, don't love. Your life is going to be misery, full of ache and regrets if you don't take action to change your job, yourself, and the balance of your life.

What are you afraid of? Do you lie alone in your bed watching the shadows dance across your wall? Do you imagine hearing footsteps or the hiss of snakes from the hallway? Do you think I might be real and creep through your house at night? Or are your fears so much more mature? You fear debt, doing without, sickness, and never realizing your dreams. Fear is an emotion that's tied to the unknown. You will never know what's going to happen, so you live in the illusion and assumption that the best and the worst will never happen to you. When you fear, when you dread the future, you're wasting time and energy.

I imagine that in your life you want the sure thing, the illusion of security, and the safest bet – which is to not to bet at all. The fear of risk, the fear of taking a chance, and the fear of failure keep you from living your life and from reaching your goals, ambitions, and finding joy, peace, and achievement. No one knows what's going to happen next. As much as you plan and work towards goals there's no telling what's going to happen. You might anticipate what's about to happen, but you don't really know the future. When you fear the unknown you're surrendering to fear before the battle's even started.

In order to get out of the job you don't want and into the circumstances you do want, you must create goals. Goals are the things and circumstances you desire for yourself, your family, and friends. They are aspirations for achievement and goals serve as motivation. Goals are things, characteristics, and accomplishments that you believe will make you a better person, happier, and will bring joy. Goals are the end result of the work, the effort, and the planning. When you think about your goals what do you think about?

Goals should not be dreamy, foggy visions of distant things, half-hearted accomplishments, and happy somedays. When you set goals you need a clear vision of what your life will become. For example, a goal to find a new job is fine, but it's not clear and precise. Goal setting only begins with a high-level objective such as finding a new job, losing weight, or running a marathon. The high-level objective of your goal demands more attention to bring it from a happy thought to an executable plan.

Once you've established your high-level goals your next process is to break down the goal into manageable chunks. Once you've broken down the goal you can begin to map activities that will bring your goal into reality. To start a new business or launch a new career is a goal that demands planning, pondering, and then executing. Nothing happens until someone does something. You can keep on in the gloom and horror of your current situation or you can get to work, real work, and make your life better. No one, not your spouse, parents, colleagues, friends, or friendly vampire can change your life for you. Where you are and where you'll be are both dependent on the actions you take.

If your job sucks, and I'm guessing it does, your vampire manager and zombie co-workers may have much to do with it. But if you stay and endure the horrors for the money your endurance brings, then there's no one to blame but yourself. Your job, your life, doesn't have to suck. You can take immediate actions to make things better. Do something that I cannot: design a life that you want to live, that will bring you joy, and create happiness for others.

Farewell

I've shared with you what I've observed and learned in my role as a vampire manager. I've seen people come from one miserable job to my employment only to resign and move onto another miserable job. I've also seen people twist and suffer for decades only to retire and die from boredom shortly thereafter. I've also seen some people learn through their observations that life is too short to be miserable. These people have learned that no amount of money, pride, and recognition is worth the unhappiness of being in the wrong job. Still others have wandered from department to department, trying to stay off my radar, drawing their paycheck, doing the minimal amount of work, and assuring themselves that this really is their good life.

I despise most of you and part of me hopes you continue to be miserable, continue to be live in fear and regret, however, there's a growing part of me that wants you to be successful. Success is unique to each person – what success is to you may not be success to me. If you want to be successful you must define what the esoteric concept of success means to you. Write down what it means to be successful, what you value, and describe your successful life. This will help you understand what you want and then it's easier to achieve.

So now I'm leaving, retiring in a way. I've had enough of the politics, the rules, the processes, forms, and endless meetings that don't matter. I'm returning to what I know how to do, what I love to do, what my purpose is in this world. Yes, even vampires have a purpose. I'm taking off this tie and these cufflinks and leaving The Organization. I'll get my own blood in my own way. I'll do it all my way – without their damned rules and procedures. It will be tough and I may soon be hunted down and staked to the earth, but at least I'll know I tried.

It's not enjoyable to be told what to do, to be lied to, and to follow someone else's way just to survive. Life is motivation enough to take action, to risk the chance to be happy, to claim a purpose in this world. I'll make you this final promise: I'll never come for you if you're happy, creating, and living a joyful life. You'll be the slim slice of the world and that's too perfect to take.

ABOUT THE AUTHOR

Joseph Phillips, PMP, Project+, CTT+, is the Director of Education for Project Seminars. He has managed and consulted on projects for various industries, including banking, technical, pharmaceutical, manufacturing, and health. He has served as a management consultant for organizations creating project offices, maturity models, and best-practice standardization.

 Mr. Phillips has taught courses for corporate clients and seminars for Columbia College, University of Chicago, Indiana University, Ball State University and others. He is a Certified Technical Trainer and has taught over 10,000 professionals and contributed as an author or editor to more than 30 books on technology, careers, project management and program management. Recent books by Joseph Phillips include:

- *Project Management for Small Business*
- *The Lifelong Project*
- *IT Project Management: On Track from Start to Finish*
- *PMP Study Guide*
- *PMP Lab Manual*
- *CAPM/PMP All-in-One Book*
- *Certified Technical Trainer+ All-in-One Book*

Phillips is a member of the Project Management Institute and is active in local project management chapters. He has spoken on project management, project management certifications, and project methodologies at numerous trade shows, PMI chapter meetings, and employee conferences. You may contact him through jdp@instructing.com.

www.ingramcontent.com/pod-product-compliance
Lightning Source LLC
Chambersburg PA
CBHW060616210326
41520CB00010B/1362